Object-Oriented Programming with PHP5

Learn to leverage PHP5's OOP features to write manageable applications with ease

Hasin Hayder

PUBLISHING

BIRMINGHAM - MUMBAI

Object-Oriented Programming with PHP5

First published: December 2007

Production Reference: 1031207

Published by Packt Publishing Ltd.
32 Lincoln Road
Olton
Birmingham, B27 6PA, UK.

ISBN 978-1-847192-56-1

www.packtpub.com

Cover Image by Karl Moore (karl.moore@ukonline.co.uk)

Credits

Author

Hasin Hayder

Reviewers

Kalpesh Barot

Murshed Ahmed Khan

Development Editor

Nanda Padmanabhan

Assistant Development Editor

Rashmi Phadnis

Technical Editor

Divya Menon

Editorial Team leader

Mithil Kulkarni

Project Manager

Abhijeet Deobhakta

Indexer

Monica Ajmera

Proofreader

Damian Carvill

Production Coordinator

Shantanu Zagade

Cover Designer

Shantanu Zagade

About the Author

Hasin Hayder is a Zend Certified Engineer and open-source enthusiast from Bangladesh. Besides his regular job as Technical Director at Trippert Labs (www.trippert.com), he is often found developing localized Bangla applications and blogging at http://hasin.wordpress.com. He lives in Bangladesh with his wife Ayesha, son Afif and plenty of toys around!

About the Reviewers

Kalpesh Barot has about 4 years of experience in the world of PHP. He has extensively worked on small and large scale social networking websites developed in PHP. He has been involved in varied projects, from planning and developing web sites to creating custom modules on big social networking websites.

Kalpesh received a Masters degree in Enterprise software Engineering from the University of Greenwich, UK in 2004. There he learned the theory behind his computer experience and became a much more efficient computer programmer.

Kalpesh has worked actively in the IT sector since his freshman year at university. He has been a PHP developer since then and has developed his skills in this field.

Through his increasing responsibilities, he has learned to prioritize needs and wants, and applies this ability to his projects.

I would like to thank my wife Bansari for her consistent support.

Murshed Ahmmad Khan is a young web developer who believes that nothing is impossible in the arena of programming. With his extensive 5 years work experience in web & system level programming he wants to create cool, applicable and useful systems for many people throughout the web.

He graduated (B.Sc. in CSE) from Rajshahi University of Engineering & Technology (RUET) Rajshahi, Bangladesh, in Computer Science & Engineering (CSE).

Murshed Ahmmad Khan worked on BangladeshInfo.com (`http://www.bangladeshinfo.com`), and Global Online Services Limited (`http://www.global.com.bd`) gaining an immense reputation. BangladeshInfo.com & Global Online Services Limited are both a concern of Texas Group Bangladesh and a renowned IT firm in the local market for corporate and multinational companies.

He also worked in THPB (The Hunger Project, Bangladesh - `http://www.thp.org`) and SHUJAN (SHUJAN is a citizen movements to achieve good governance) as a lead developer for developing various e-governance sites for increasing the accountability of the candidates of national elections. From SHUJAN (`http://www.shujan.org`) he also developed the country's first ever online.

Table of Contents

Introduction

Object-oriented programming is largely about the ability to hide what's not important to the user and to highlight what is. PHP 5 offers standardized means for specifying the variety of property scopes typically offered by full-featured OO languages.

What This Book Covers

Chapter 1 introduces object-oriented programming and how it fits for PHP. Some benefits of functional programming over procedural programming are highlighted.

In *Chapter 2* you learn to create objects and define their properties and methods. Details of classes, properties, and methods follow, along with the scope of methods. This chapter shows you the benefits of using interfaces and a few other basic OOP features in PHP to kick start your journey through OOPing in PHP.

Now that you have got your basics done for OOP in PHP, *Chapter 3* helps you to strengthen your base. It helps you to deal with more details and some advanced features. For example, you learn about class information functions, which allows you to investigate details of any class. This chapter takes you through some handy object-oriented information functions, exception handling, iterators, and storing objects using serialization.

In *Chapter 4* you learn some of the Design Patterns and how to implement them in PHP. These are an essential part of OOP and make your code more effective, more efficient, and easier to maintain. Sometimes we implement these design patterns in our code without knowing that these solutions are defined by design patterns. Proper usage of the correct pattern can make your code perform better; similarly using them improperly could make your code slower and less efficient.

Chapter 5 focuses on two very important features of object-oriented programming in PHP, reflection and unit testing. PHP5 replaces many old APIs with smarter new ones. One of these is the Reflection API, with which you can reverse or engineer any class or object to figure out its properties and methods. You can invoke those methods dynamically and more. Unit testing is an essential part of good, stable, and manageable application design. We focus on one very popular package, PHPUnit, which is a port of JUnit to PHP. If you follow the guidelines provided in this chapter you will be able to design your own unit tests successfully.

Some built-in objects and interfaces in PHP make life much easier for PHP developers. In *Chapter 6* you will learn about the huge object repository named the Standard PHP Library or SPL.

Chapter 7: In this chapter we discuss the improved MySQL API known as MySQLi and take a basic look at PHP Data Objects (PDO), adoDB, and PEAR::MDB2. We take a look at the Active Record pattern in PHP using adoDB's active record library and the Object-Relational Mapping (ORM) pattern using Propel. We focus on some specific topics that are interesting for PHP developers doing database access the OO way.

In *Chapter 8*, you learn to process XML with PHP. You get to know about different APIs like the SimpleXML API to read XML and the DOMDocument object to parse and create XML documents.

Chapter 9: In Chapter 4 you learned how design patterns can simplify your daily life in programming by providing you with a common approach for solving problems. One of the most used design patterns for application architecture is Model-View-Controller (MVC). In this chapter we discuss the basic structure of MVC frameworks and then introduce you to some of these popular frameworks. Frameworks play a very important role in Rapid Development of PHP applications. You will learn how to build a framework in this chapter, which will also help you to understand object loading, data abstraction layers, and the importance of separation and finally you get a closer look at how applications are done.

Who is This Book for

From beginners to intermediate users of PHP5

Conventions

In this book, you will find a number of styles of text that distinguish between different kinds of information. Here are some examples of these styles, and an explanation of their meaning.

There are three styles for code. Code words in text are shown as follows: "In some cases you may need to investigate which classes are in the current scope. You can do it easily with `get_declared_classes()` function."

A block of code will be set as follows:

```
<?
class ParentClass
{
}
class ChildClass extends ParentClass
{
}
$cc = new ChildClass();
if  (is_a($cc,"ChildClass")) echo "It's a ChildClass Type Object";
echo "\n";
if  (is_a($cc,"ParentClass")) echo "It's also a ParentClass Type
Object";
?>
```

New terms and **important words** are introduced in a bold-type font. Words that you see on the screen, in menus or dialog boxes for example, appear in our text like this: " If you place the server in your web server (here `localhost`) document, root in a folder named `proxy` and then access the client, you will get the following output:

March, 28 2007 16:13:20".

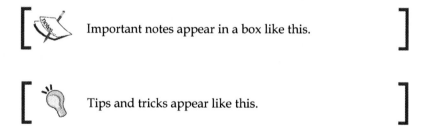

Important notes appear in a box like this.

Tips and tricks appear like this.

Reader Feedback

Feedback from our readers is always welcome. Let us know what you think about this book, what you liked or may have disliked. Reader feedback is important for us to develop titles that you really get the most out of.

To send us general feedback, simply drop an email to `feedback@packtpub.com`, making sure to mention the book title in the subject of your message.

If there is a book that you need and would like to see us publish, please send us a note in the **SUGGEST A TITLE** form on `www.packtpub.com` or email `suggest@packtpub.com`.

If there is a topic that you have expertise in and you are interested in either writing or contributing to a book, see our author guide on `www.packtpub.com/authors`.

Customer Support

Now that you are the proud owner of a Packt book, we have a number of things to help you to get the most from your purchase.

Downloading the Example Code for the Book

Visit `http://www.packtpub.com/files/code/2561_Code.zip`, and select this book from the list of titles to download any example code or extra resources for this book. The files available for download will then be displayed.

The downloadable files contain instructions on how to use them.

Errata

Although we have taken every care to ensure the accuracy of our contents, mistakes do happen. If you find a mistake in one of our books—maybe a mistake in text or code—we would be grateful if you would report this to us. By doing this you can save other readers from frustration, and help to improve subsequent versions of this book. If you find any errata, report them by visiting `http://www.packtpub.com/support`, selecting your book, clicking on the **Submit Errata** link, and entering the details of your errata. Once your errata are verified, your submission will be accepted and the errata are added to the list of existing errata. The existing errata can be viewed by selecting your title from `http://www.packtpub.com/support`.

Questions

You can contact us at `questions@packtpub.com` if you are having a problem with some aspect of the book, and we will do our best to address it.

*This book is dedicated to
my Son
Afif – The Little Einstein*

1
OOP vs. Procedural Programming

PHP is one of the most popular scripting languages of the last couple of years. Almost 60% of web servers are running on Apache with PHP. It is so popular that millions of websites and web applications are developed every month using PHP. PHP started its journey as a simple replacement for Perl, and in a few years it became tremendously popular and powerful. The language itself is closely similar to ANSI C.

One of the reasons why PHP became so popular is its short learning curve. Learning PHP is not a big job, especially if you are familiar with the syntax of Java or C. As writing PHP scripts is easy, anyone can write PHP code without following conventions and mixing presentation layers with business logics (which is one of the main reasons why there are large amounts of unmanageable projects floating around). Because there are no strict coding conventions followed in PHP, over the years as a project gets bigger, it can turn into an unmanageable demon.

OOP or **Object Oriented Programming** is a good programming practise to create manageable projects more easily. Procedural programming means writing code without objects. Procedural programming consists of codes with or without routines. OOP enlightens any language for better coding, for best performance and for writing very big projects without worrying a lot about managing them. OOP gives you facilities to create reusable objects that you or other developers can use in their projects without reinventing them again and again. OOP removes the hassles and difficulties of writing and managing big applications.

In this book we are going to discuss how you can achieve maximum benefits using OOP with PHP, using step-by-step instructions, real life examples how OOP helps you to write effective code, how to improve your coding style, and how to reuse them over time. This book won't work as a reference for PHP language; we will just cover OOP features of PHP and not the basics of general PHP. If you are looking for a good reference book, consult the PHP manual at first and then you can study *Core PHP Programming*, a very good book written by Leon Atkinson.

Introduction to PHP

This section is not for you if you are already a PHP developer, but for those who are new to PHP and starting with this book. Though I said at the very beginning that I assume you will have some pre development experience in PHP while reading this book, but if you are a total fresher and want to learn OOP with this book, this section may be worth recalling the basic PHP language features. If you are already familiar enough, don't skip this section as we have other topics to discuss here.

So you may ask where is the introduction to PHP, I am not seeing any code here! Well, you don't need to. The best resource on the internet is for free. Please go to http://www.php.net and download the manual and read the basic chapters. For a detailed learning of PHP, you can study the book *Learning PHP5* written by David Sklar.

Ready, Set, Go

In this book, we are using PHP5.1.2 for our examples but for almost 99% of cases it will run with PHP version 5x. We have MySQL 5 in our machine and Apache 2 as our web server. If you aren't familiar with configuring all these in your machine, you can download pre configured WAMP or LAMP distributions like XAMPP (http://apachefriends.org) or Apache2Triad (http://www.apache2triad.net). You will find corresponding documentation for installation and customization on each of these product's website.

A Little History of OOP in PHP

When PHP was developed, it did not implement OO features in itself. After PHP/FI, when Zeev, Rasmus, and Andy rewrote the core and released PHP3, very basic OO features were introduced. When PHP4 was released, OO features got matured with huge performance improvement. But the PHP team rewrote the core engine again to introduce completely new object models and released PHP5. Now there are two versions of PHP being developed. Don't get confused by comparing PHP versions with other languages. PHP5 doesn't mean it is the latest PHP version. As I said a while ago, PHP4 and PHP5 are being released actively (though there will be no more releases of PHP4 after December 2007). Between these two, PHP5 implements almost complete OO features while PHP4 doesn't. At the time of writing this book the latest version of these two streams are PHP5.2 and PHP4.4.

Procedural vs. OO Coding Style

PHP allows you to write code in two flavours, one is procedural and the other is object oriented. You can even write procedural code in PHP5 and it will run without any problems. If you are not clear about procedural and object oriented programming, then we will have a look at these two different coding styles. The following two examples are not fully running examples rather a pseudo code:

```php
<?
$user_input = $_POST['field'];
$filtered_content = filter($user_input); //user input filtering
mysql_connect("dbhost","dbuser","dbpassword"); //database
mysql_select_db("dbname");
$sql = "some query";
$result = mysql_query($sql);
while ($data = mysql_fetch_assoc())
{
   process ($data);
}
process_user_input($filtered_content);
?>
```

You will notice using a lot of inline processing either directly or via using functions. It may stand as an example of typical procedural operation. Let's see how it looks after converting it to OOP:

```php
<?
$input_filter = new filter();
$input_filter->filter_user_input(); //filter the user inputs
$db = new dal("mysql"); //data access layer
$db->connect($dbconfig);//we wre using mysql
$result = $db->execute($sql);
ReportGenerator::makereport($result); //process data
$model = new Postmodel($filter->get_filtered_content());
$model->insert();
?>
```

Now if you take a look into these two code snippets, you will find that the latter one is much more readable. Well, you can make the first one more readable by introducing some more functions into it, but how many functions are you ready to search into when you use them? The latter snippet is better organized because you know which object is handling which process. If you write big applications in procedural style, it will be almost impossible to manage after a few versions. Of course you can implement strict coding conventions, but it is agreed by millions of developers that it won't give you the ultimate manageability and usability if it's procedural unless you do it in OO style. Almost all big applications are written using the object oriented approach.

Benefits of OOP

OOP is invented to make the developer's life easier. Using OOP you can split your problems into smaller problems that are comparatively easy to comprehend. The main goal of OOP is: everything you want to do, do it via objects. Objects are basically small discrete pieces of code which, can incorporate data and behaviors together. In an application all these objects are connected to each other, they share data among them and solve problems.

OOP can be considered better from many aspects, especially when you consider the development time and maintenance overhead. The main benefits of OOP can be considered as follows:

- **Reusability**: An object is an entity which has bundles of properties and methods and can interact with other objects. An object can be sufficient or it may have dependencies over other objects. But an object is usually developed to solve a specific set of problems. So when other developers suffer from the same set of problems, they can just incorporate your class to their project and use it without affecting their existing workflow. It prevents from DRY, which means *Don't Repeat Yourself*. In functional or modular programming, reusing is possible but complex.

- **Refactoring**: When you need to refactor your projects, OOP gives you the maximum benefit because all objects are small entities and contain its properties and methods as a part of itself. So refactoring is comparatively easier.

- **Extensible**: If you need to add features to your project, you can achieve best results from OOP. One of the core OOP features is extensibility. You can refactor your object to add the feature. While doing it, you can still maintain backward compatibility of this object so that it works fine with an old code base. Or you can extend the object and create a totally new object that retains all the necessary properties and methods of the parent object from which it has been derived, and then expose new features. This is termed "inheritance" and is a very important feature of OOP.

- **Maintenance**: Object oriented code is easier to maintain because it follows somewhat strict coding conventions and is written in a self explanatory format. For example, when a developer extends it, refactors it, or debugs it, they can easily find out the inner coding structure and maintain the code time after time. Moreover, whenever there is a team development environment in your project, OOP could be the best solution because you can distribute your code after splitting it into small parts. These small parts could be developed as a separate object, so developers can develop them almost independently. Finally, it will be very easy to merge the code.

- **Efficiency**: The concept of object oriented programming is actually developed for better efficiency and ease of development process. Several design patterns are developed to create better and efficient code. Moreover in OOP, you can think of your solution in a much better approach than procedural programming. Because you first split your problem into a small set of problems and then find solutions for each of them, the big problem is solved automatically.

Dissection of an Object

So what is an object? Well, it's nothing but a piece of code with a bunch of properties and methods. So is it similar to an array, as arrays can store data identified by properties (well, they are called keys)? Objects are much more than arrays because they contain some methods inside them. They can either hide them or expose them, which are not possible in arrays. The object is somewhat comparable with a data structure, data structure, and can incorporate a lot of other objects in itself and either creates a tight coupling among them or a loose one. And object can incorporate a lot of other object in itself and either creates a tight coupling among them or a loose one. We will learn more about loose coupling and tight coupling later in this book and understand how they will be useful for us.

Let's see the code of an object in PHP. The following object is a very simple object which can send email to a bunch of users. In PHP5, objects are a lot more different than an object in PHP4. We will not discuss the details of it, this is just an introductory object to see how the objects are written in PHP.

```php
<?
//class.emailer.php
class emailer
{
  private $sender;
  private $recipients;
  private $subject;
  private $body;
  function __construct($sender)
  {
    $this->sender = $sender;
    $this->recipients = array();
  }

  public function addRecipients($recipient)
  {
    array_push($this->recipients, $recipient);
  }
```

```php
      public function setSubject($subject)
      {
         $this->subject = $subject;
      }
      public function setBody($body)
      {
         $this->body = $body;
      }
      public function sendEmail()
      {
         foreach ($this->recipients as $recipient)
         {
            $result = mail($recipient, $this->subject, $this->body,
                                "From: {$this->sender}\r\n");
            if ($result) echo "Mail successfully sent to
                                        {$recipient}<br/>";
         }
      }
   }
?>
```

The above object contains four private properties and three accessor methods and finally one more method to dispose the email to recipients. So how we are going to use it in our PHP code? Let's see below:

```php
<?
$emailer = new emailer("hasin@pageflakes.com"); //construcion
$emailer->addRecipients("hasin@somewherein.net"); //accessing methods
// and passing some data
$emailer->setSubject("Just a Test");
$emailer->setBody("Hi Hasin, How are you?");
$emailer->sendEmail();
?>
```

I am sure that the above code snippet is much more self explanatory and readable. If you follow proper conventions, you can make your code easy to manage and maintain. Wordpress developers use a motto on their site www.wordpress.org which is "Coding is poetry". Coding is exactly a poem; if you just know how to write it.

Difference of OOP in PHP4 and PHP5

Objects in PHP5 differ a lot from objects in PHP4. OOP became matured enough in true sense from PHP5. OOP was introduced since PHP3 but that was just an illusion for real object oriented programming. In PHP4 you can create objects but you can't feel the real flavour of an object there. In PHP4 it was almost a poor object model.

One of the main differences of OOP in PHP4 is that everything is open; no restrictions about the usage of methods or properties. You can't use public, private, and protected modifiers for your methods. In PHP4 developers usually declare private methods with a double underscore. But it doesn't mean that declaring a method in that format actually prevents you from accessing that method outside the class. It's just a discipline followed.

In PHP4 you can find interfaces but no abstract or final keyword. An interface is a piece of code that any object can implement and that means the object must have all the methods declared in the interface. It strictly checks that you must implement all the functions in it. In the interface you can only declare the name and the access type of any method. An abstract class is where some methods may have some body too. Then any object can extend that abstract class and extend all these methods defined in that abstract class. A final class is an object which you are not allowed to extend. In PHP5 you can use all of these.

In PHP4 there are no multiple inheritances for interfaces. That means an interface can extend only one interface. But in PHP5 multiple inheritance is supported via implementing multiple interfaces together.

In PHP4, almost everything is static. That means if you declare any method in the class, you can call it directly without creating an instance of it. For example the following piece of code is valid in PHP4:

```
<?
class Abc
{
  var $ab;
  function abc()
  {
    $this->ab = 7;
  }
  function echosomething()
  {
    echo $this->ab;
  }
}
echo abc::echosomething();
?>
```

However it is not valid in PHP5 because the method `echosomething()` uses `$this` keyword which is not available in a static call.

There is no class-based constant in PHP4. There is no static property in objects in PHP4, and there is no destructor in PHP4 objects.

Whenever an object is copied, it is a shallow copy of that object. But in PHP5 shallow copy is possible only using the clone keyword.

There is no exception object in PHP4. But in PHP5 exception management is a great added feature.

There were some functions to investigate methods and properties of a class in PHP4, but in PHP5 beside those functions, a powerful set of API (Reflection API) is introduced for this purpose.

Method overloading via magic methods like `__get()` and `__set()` are available in PHP5. There are also lots of built-in objects to make your life easier.

But most of all, there is a huge performance improvement in PHP5 for OOP.

Some Basic OO Terms

Some of the basic object-oriented terms are as follows:

Class: A class is a template for an object. A class contains the code which defines how an object will behave and interact either with each other, or with it. Every time you create an object in PHP, you are actually developing the class. So sometimes in this book we will name an object as `class`, as they are both synonymous.

Property: A property is a container inside the class which can retain some information. Unlike other languages, PHP doesn't check the type of property variable. A property could be accessible only in class itself, by its subclass, or by everyone. In essence, a property is a variable which is declared inside the class itself, but not inside any function in that class.

Method: Methods are functions inside a class. Like properties, methods can also be accessible by those three types of users.

Encapsulation: Encapsulation is the mechanism that binds together code and the data it manipulates, and keeps both safe from outside interference and misuse. The wrapping up of data and methods into a single unit (called class) is known as encapsulation. The benefit of encapsulating is that it performs the task inside without making you worry.

Polymorphism: Objects could be of any type. A discrete object can have discrete properties and methods which work separately to other objects. However a set of objects could be derived from a parent object and retain some properties of the parent class. This process is called polymorphism. An object could be morphed into several other objects retaining some of its behaviour.

Inheritance: The key process of deriving a new object by extending another object is called inheritance. When you inherit an object from another object, the subclass (which inherits) derives all the properties and methods of the superclass (which is inherited). A subclass can then process each method of superclass anyway (which is called overriding).

Coupling: Coupling is the behaviour of how classes are dependent on each other. Loosely coupled architecture is much more reusable than tightly coupled objects. In the next chapter we will learn details about coupling. Coupling is a very important concern for designing better objects.

Design Patterns: First invented by the "Gang of Four", design patterns are just tricks in object oriented programming to solve similar sets of problems with a smarter approach. Using design patterns (DP) can increase the performance of your whole application with minimal code written by developers. Sometimes it is not possible to design optimized solutions without using DP. But unnecessary and unplanned use of DP can also degrade the performance of your application. We have a chapter devoted for design patterns in this book.

Subclass: A very common term in OOP, and we use this term throughout this book. When an object is derived from another object, the derived one is called the subclass of which it is derived from.

Superclass: A class is superclass to an object if that object is derived from it. To keep it simple, when you extend an object, the object which you are extending is the superclass of a newly extended object.

Instance: Whenever you create an object by calling its constructor, it will be called an instance. To simplify this, whenever you write some thing like this `$var = new Object();` you actually create an instance of object class.

General Coding Conventions

We will be following some conventions in our codes throughout the book. Not being too strict, these conventions will help you to maintain your application at a large extent. Also, it will increase the maintainability of your code. It will also help you to write efficient code by avoiding duplicity and redundant objects. Last but not least, it will make your code much more readable.

- In a single php file, we never write more than one class at a time. Out of the scope of that class, we will not write any procedural code.

- We will save any class with a proper naming convention. For example we will save the file where we place the `Emailer` class introduced earlier in this chapter as `class.emailer.php`. What benefits can you achieve using this naming convention? Well, without going inside that file, you are now at least confirmed that this file contains a class named "Emailer".

- Never mix the case in filenames. It creates ugly application structure. Go ahead with all small letters.

- Like classes, we will save any interface as `interface.name.php`, Abstract class as `abstract.name.php`, and Final class as `final.name.php`.

- We will always use Camel case while naming our classes. And that means the first letters of the major part is always a capital letter and the rest are small letter. For example a class named "arrayobject" will be more readable if we write `ArrayObject`.

- While writing the name of properties or class variables, we will follow the same convention.

- While writing the name of a method, we will start with a small letter and then the rest are camel case. For example, a method to send an email could be named as `sendEmail`.

- Well, there is no more conventions used in this book.

Summary

In this chapter we learned about the object oriented programming and how it fits in with PHP. We have also learned some benefits over procedural and functional programming. However, we haven't gone through the details of OO language in PHP. In the next chapter we will learn more about objects and their methods and attributes, specifically creating objects, extending its features, and interacting between them. So, let our journey begin, Happy OOPing with PHP.

2
Kick-Starting OOP

In this chapter we will learn how to create objects, define their attributes (or properties) and methods. Objects in PHP are always created using a "class" keyword. In this chapter we will learn the details of classes, properties, and methods. We will also learn the scope of methods and about modifiers and the benefits of using interfaces This chapter will also introduce us to other basic OOP features in PHP. As a whole, this chapter is one of the better resources for you to kick-start OOP in PHP.

Let's Bake Some Objects

As I said before, you can create an object in PHP using the class keyword. A class consists of some properties and methods, either public or private. Let's take the Emailer class that we have seen in our first chapter. We will discuss here what it actually does:

```php
<?
//class.emailer.php
class Emailer
{
  private $sender;
  private $recipients;
  private $subject;
  private $body;
  function __construct($sender)
  {
    $this->sender = $sender;
    $this->recipients = array();
  }
  public function addRecipients($recipient)
  {
```

```
      array_push($this->recipients, $recipient);
   }
   public function setSubject($subject)
   {
      $this->subject = $subject;
   }
   public function setBody($body)
   {
      $this->body = $body;
   }
   public function sendEmail()
   {
   foreach ($this->recipients as $recipient)
   {
      $result = mail($recipient, $this->subject, $this->body,
                          "From: {$this->sender}\r\n");
      if ($result) echo "Mail successfully sent to {$recipient}<br/>";
      }
   }
}
?>
```

In this code, we started with class Emailer, which means that the name of our class is Emailer. While naming a class, follow the same naming convention as variables, i.e. you can't start with a numeric letter, etc.

After that we declared the properties of this class. There are four properties here, namely, $sender, $recipient, $subject, and $body. Please note that we declare each of them with a keyword private. A private property means that this property can only be accessed internally from this class. Properties are nothing but variables inside a class.

If you remember what a method is, it is just a function inside the class. In this class there are five functions, __construct(), addRecipient(), setSubject(), setBody(), and sendEmail(). Please note that the last four methods are declared public. That means when someone instantiates this object, they can access these methods.

The __construct() is a special method inside a class which is called constructor method. Whenever a new object is created from this class, this method will execute automatically. So if we have to perform some preliminary tasks in our object while initiating it, we will do from this constructor method. For example, in the constructor method of this Emailer class we just set the $recipients as a blank array and we also set the sender name.

Accessing Properties and Methods from Inside the Class

Are you wondering how a function can access the class properties from inside its content? Let's see using the following code:

```
public function setBody($body)
{
   $this->body = $body;
}
```

There is a private property named $body inside our class, and if we want to access it from within the function, we must refer to it with $this. $this means a reference to current instance of this object. So we can access the body property with $this->body. Please note that we have to access the properties (i.e class variables) of a class using a "->" following the instance.

Similarly, like properties, we can access any member method from inside another member method in this format. For example, we can evoke setSubject method as $this->setSubject().

Please note that $this keyword is only valid inside the scope of a method, as long as it is not declared as static. You can not use $this keyword from outside the class. We will learn about this "static", "private", "public" keywords more in the *Modifiers* section later this chapter.

Using an Object

Let's use the newly created Emailer object from inside our PHP code. We must note some things before using an object. You must initiate an object before using it. After initiating, you can access all its public properties and methods using "->" after the instance. Let's see using the following code:

```
<?
$emailerobject = new Emailer("hasin@pageflakes.com");
$emailerobject->addRecipients("hasin@somewherein.net");
$emailerobject->setSubject("Just a Test");
$emailerobject->setBody("Hi Hasin, How are you?");
$emailerobject->sendEmail();
?>
```

In the above code piece, we first created an instance of `Emailer` class to a variable name `$emailerobject` in the first line. Here, there is something important to note: We are supplying a sender address while instantiating this:

```
$emailerobject = new Emailer("hasin@pageflakes.com");
```

Remember we had a constructor method in our class as `__construct($sender)`. When initiating an object, we said that the constructor method is called automatically. So while initiating this `Emailer` class we must supply the proper arguments as declared in the constructor method. For example the following code will create a warning:

```
<?
$emailer = new emailer();
?>
```

When you execute the above code, it shows the warning as follows:

```
Warning: Missing argument 1 for emailer::__construct(),
called in C:\OOP with PHP5\Codes\ch1\class.emailer.php on line 42
and defined in <b>C:\OOP with PHP5\Codes\ch1\class.emailer.php</b>
on line <b>9</b><br />
```

See the difference? If your class had no constructor method or a constructor with no arguments, you can instantiate it with the above code.

Modifiers

You have seen that we used some keywords like `private` or `public` in our class. So what are these and why do we need to use them? Well, these keywords are called modifier and introduced in PHP5. They were *not* available in PHP4. These keywords help you to define how these variables and properties will be accessed by the user of this class. Let's see what these modifiers actually do.

Private: Properties or methods declared as private are not allowed to be called from outside the class. However any method inside the same class can access them without a problem. In our `Emailer` class we have all these properties declared as private, so if we execute the following code we will find an error.

```
<?
include_once("class.emailer.php");
$emobject = new Emailer("hasin@somewherein.net");
$emobject->subject = "Hello world";
?>
```

The above code upon execution gives a fatal error as shown below:

```
<b>Fatal error</b>: Cannot access private property emailer::$subject
 in <b>C:\OOP with PHP5\Codes\ch1\class.emailer.php</b> on line
<b>43</b></br />
```

That means you can't access any private property or method from outside the class.

Public: Any property or method which is not explicitly declared as private or protected is a public method. You can access a public method from inside or outside the class.

Protected: This is another modifier which has a special meaning in OOP. If any property or method is declared as protected, you can only access the method from its subclass. We will learn details about subclass later in this chapter. But to see how a protected method or property actually works, we'll use the following example:

To start, let's open `class.emailer.php` file (the `Emailer` class) and change the declaration of the `$sender` variable. Make it as follows:

```
protected $sender
```

Now create another file name `class.extendedemailer.php` with the following code:

```php
<?
class ExtendedEmailer extends emailer
{
function  __construct(){}
  public function setSender($sender)
  {
    $this->sender = $sender;
  }
}
?>
```

Now use this object like this:

```php
<?
include_once("class.emailer.php");
include_once("class.extendedemailer.php");
$xemailer = new ExtendedEmailer();
$xemailer->setSender("hasin@pageflakes.com");
$xemailer->addRecipients("hasin@somewherein.net");
$xemailer->setSubject("Just a Test");
$xemailer->setBody("Hi Hasin, How are you?");
$xemailer->sendEmail();
?>
```

Now if you look carefully at the code of the ExtendedEmailer class, you will find that we accessed the $sender property of its parent (which is actually Emailer class). We have been able to access that property only because it was declared as protected. One more benefit we get here, is that the property $sender is still inaccessible directly from outside the scope of these two classes. That means if we execute the following code, it will generate a fatal error.

```
<?
include_once("class.emailer.php");
include_once("class.extendedmailer.php");
$xemailer = new ExtendedEmailer();
$xemailer->sender = "hasin@pageflakes.com";
?>
```

Upon execution, it gives the following error:

```
<b>Fatal error</b>:  Cannot access protected property
extendedEmailer::$sender in <b>C:\OOP with
PHP5\Codes\ch1\test.php</b> on line <b>5</b><br />
```

Constructors and Destructors

We discussed earlier in this chapter about the constructor method. A constructor method is the method that executes automatically while creating instances of the class. In PHP5, there are two ways you can write a constructor method inside a class. The first one is to create a method with the name __construct() inside the class. The second is to create a method naming exactly the same as class name. For example if your class name is Emailer, the name of the constructor method will be Emailer(). Let's take a look at the following class which calculates the factorial of any number:

```
<?
//class.factorial.php
class factorial
{
  private $result = 1;// you can initialize directly outside
  private $number;
  function __construct($number)
  {
    $this->number = $number;
    for($i=2; $i<=$number; $i++)
    {
      $this->result *= $i;
    }
  }
```

```
  public function showResult()
  {
    echo "Factorial of {$this->number} is {$this->result}. ";
  }
}
?>
```

In the code above, we used __construct() as our constructor function. The behaviour will be same if you rename the __construct() function as factorial().

Now, you may ask if a class can have constructors in both styles? This means a function named __construct() and a function named the same as class name. So which constructor will execute, or will they both execute? This is a good question. Actually there is no chance of executing both. If there is a constructor in both styles, PHP5 will give preference to the __construct() function and the other one will be ignored. Let's take a look using the following example

```
<?
//class.factorial.php
class Factorial
{
  private $result = 1;
  private $number;
  function __construct($number)
  {
    $this->number = $number;
    for($i=2; $i<=$number; $i++)
    {
      $this->result*=$i;
    }
    echo "__construct() executed. ";
  }
  function factorial($number)
  {
    $this->number = $number;
    for($i=2; $i<=$number; $i++)
    {
      $this->result*=$i;
    }
    echo "factorial() executed. ";
  }
  public function showResult()
  {
    echo "Factorial of {$this->number} is {$this->result}. ";
  }
}
?>
```

Now if you use this class as shown below:

```
<?
include_once("class.factorial.php");
$fact = new Factorial(5);
$fact->showResult();
?>
```

You will find that the output is:

```
__construct() executed. Factorial of 5 is 120
```

Similar to the constructor method, there is a **destructor** method which actually works upon destroying an object. You can explicitly create a destructor method by naming it __destruct(). This method will be invoked automatically by PHP at the end of the execution of your script. To test this, let's add the following code in our factorial class:

```
function __destruct()
{
   echo " Object Destroyed.";
}
```

Now execute the usage script again, you will see the following output this time:

```
__construct() executed. Factorial of 5 is 120. Object Destroyed.
```

Class Constants

Hopefully, you will already know that you can create constants in your PHP scripts using the **define** keyword to define (constant name, constant value). But to create constants in the class you have to use the const keyword. These constants actually work like static variables, the only difference is that they are read-only. Let's see how we can create constants and use them:

```
<?
class WordCounter
{
   const ASC=1;   //you need not use $ sign before Constants
   const DESC=2;
   private $words;
   function __construct($filename)
   {
     $file_content = file_get_contents($filename);
     $this->words =
           (array_count_values(str_word_count(strtolower
                                     ($file_content),1)));
```

```
        }
    public function count($order)
    {
        if ($order==self::ASC)
        asort($this->words);
        else if($order==self::DESC)
        arsort($this->words);
        foreach ($this->words as $key=>$val)
        echo $key ." = ". $val."<br/>";
    }
}
?>
```

This `WordCounter` class counts the frequency of words in any given file. Here we define two constant names ASC and DESC whose values are 1 and 2 respectively. To access these constants from within the class, we reference them with the `self` keyword. Please note that we are accessing them with the `::` operator, not a `->` operator, because these constants act like a static member.

Finally to use this class, let's create a snippet as shown below. In this snippet we are also accessing those constants:

```
<?
include_once("class.wordcounter.php");
$wc = new WordCounter("words.txt");
$wc->count(WordCounter::DESC);
?>
```

Please note that we are accessing the class constants from outside the class by following the `::` operator right after the class name, not after the instance of the class. Now let's test the script, please create a file named `words.txt` with the following content in the same directory where you placed the above script:

```
words.txt
Wordpress is an open source blogging engine. If you are not familiar
  with blogging, it is something like keeping a diary on the web.
A blog stands for web log. Wordpress is totally free and
released under the GPL.
```

Now, if you execute the usage script, this time, you will see the following output.

```
is = 3
a = 2
blogging = 2
web = 2
wordpress = 2
```

```
stands = 1
blog = 1
in = 1
diary = 1
for = 1
free = 1
under = 1
gpl = 1
released = 1
and = 1
totally = 1
log = 1
something = 1
if = 1
you = 1
engine = 1
source = 1
an= 1
open = 1
are = 1
not = 1
ï = 1
like = 1
it = 1
with = 1
familiar = 1
keeping = 1
```

Nice utility, what do you think?

Extending a Class [Inheritance]

One of the greatest features in OOP is that you can extend a class and create a
completely new object. The new object can retain all the functionality of the parent
object from which it is extended or can override. The new object can also introduce
some features. Let's extend our `Emailer` class and override the `sendEmail` function
so that it can send HTML mails.

```
<?
class HtmlEmailer extends emailer
{
  public function sendHTMLEmail()
  {
    foreach ($this->recipients as $recipient)
```

```
    {
      $headers   = 'MIME-Version: 1.0' . "\r\n";
      $headers  .= 'Content-type: text/html; charset=iso-8859-1' .
                                                      "\r\n";
      $headers  .= 'From: {$this->sender}' . "\r\n";
      $result = mail($recipient, $this->subject, $this->body,
                                               $headers);
      if ($result) echo "HTML Mail successfully sent to
                                           {$recipient}<br/>";
    }
  }
}
?>
```

As this class extends the `Emailer` class and introduces a new function, `sendHTMLEmail()`, you can still have all the methods from its parent. That means the following code is fully valid:

```
<?
include_once("class.htmlemailer.php");
$hm = new HtmlEmailer();
//.... do other things
$hm->sendEmail();
$hm->sendHTMLEmail();
?>
```

If you want to access any method of the parent class (or you may say superclass) from which it is derived, you can call using the `parent` keyword. For example, if you want to access a method named `sayHello`, you should write `parent::sayHello();`

Please note that we didn't write any function named `sendEmail()` in `HtmlEmailer` class, but that method is working from its parent, `Emailer` class.

In the above example, `HtmlEmailer` is a subclass of `Emailer` class and `Emailer` class is a superclass of `HtmlEmailer`. You must remember that if the subclass has no constructor in it, the constructor from superclass will be invoked. At the time of writing this book, there is no support for multiple inheritances at class level. This means you can't extend more than one class at a time. However multiple inheritance is supported in interfaces. An interface can extend an arbitrary number of other interfaces at a time.

Overriding Methods

In an extended object you can override any method (either declared as protected or public) and perform anything as you wish. So how can you override any method? Simply create a function with the same name that you want to override. For example, if you create a function name `sendEmail` in `HtmlEmailer` class, it will override the `sendEmail()` method of its parent, `Emailer` class. If you declare any variable in subclass which is also available in superclass, then when you access that variable, the one from subclass will be accessed.

Preventing from Overriding

If you declare any method as a `final` method, it can't be overridden in any of its subclass. So if you don't want someone to override your class methods, declare it as final. Let's take a look at the following example:

```
<?
class SuperClass
{
  public final function someMethod()
  {
    //..something here
  }
}
class SubClass extends SuperClass
{
  public function someMethod()
  {
    //..something here again, but it wont run
  }
}
?>
```

If you execute the above code, it will generate a fatal error because class `SubClass` tried to override a method in `SuperClass` which was declared as `final`.

Preventing from Extending

Similar to a final method, you can declare a class as final, which will prevent anyone from extending it. So if you declare any class, as shown in following example, it is no more extensible.

```
<?
final class aclass
{
```

```
}

class bclass extends aclass
{
}
?>
```

If you execute the code above, it will trigger the following error:

```
<b>Fatal error</b>:  Class bclass may not inherit from final class
(aclass) in <b>C:\OOP with PHP5\Codes\ch1\class.aclass.php</b> on
line <b>8</b><br />
```

Polymorphism

As we explained before, polymorphism is the process of creating several objects from specific base classes. For example, take a look at the following case in point. We need the three classes that we created earlier in this chapter, `Emailer`, `ExtendedEmailer` and `HtmlEmailer`. Let's take a look at the following code.

```
<?
include("class.emailer.php");
include("class.extendedemailer.php");
include("class.htmlemailer.php");

$emailer = new Emailer("hasin@somewherein.net");
$extendedemailer = new ExtendedEmailer();
$htmlemailer = new HtmlEmailer("hasin@somewherein.net");
if ($extendedemailer instanceof emailer  )
echo "Extended Emailer is Derived from Emailer.<br/>";
if ($htmlemailer instanceof emailer  )
echo "HTML Emailer is also Derived from Emailer.<br/>";
if ($emailer instanceof htmlEmailer )
echo "Emailer is Derived from HTMLemailer.<br/>";
if ($htmlemailer instanceof extendedEmailer  )
echo "HTML Emailer is Derived from Emailer.<br/>";
?>
```

If you execute the script above, you will find the following output:

```
Extended Emailer is Derived from Emailer.
HTML Emailer is also Derived from Emailer.
```

This is an example of polymorphism.

 You can always check if a class is derived from another class by using the instanceof operator.

Interface

Interface is an empty class which contains only the declaration of methods. So any class which implements this interface must contain the declared functions in it. So, interface is nothing but a strict ruling, which helps to extend any class and strictly implement all methods defined in interface. A class can use any interface by using the implements keyword. Please note that in interface you can only declare methods, but you cannot write their body. That means the body of all methods must remain blank.

So why is an interface necessary, you might ask? One of the reasons is it implies strict rules while creating a class. For example, we know that we need to create some driver classes in our application, which can handle DB operations. For MySQL, there will be one class, for PostgreSQL there will be another, For SQLite, another one and so forth. Now your developer team has three developers, who will separately create these three classes.

Now how will it be if each of them implements their own style in their own classes? The developers who are going to use those driver classes will have to check how they define their methods and following that, the way they have to write their code, which is too boring and hard to maintain. So if you define that, all driver class must have two methods named connect() and execute(). Now developers need not worry while changing the driver, because they know that all these classes have the same method definition. Interface helps in this scenario. Let's create the interface here:

```
<?
//interface.dbdriver.php
interface DBDriver
{
  public function connect();
  public function execute($sql);
}
?>
```

Did you notice that the functions are empty in an interface? Now let's create our `MySQLDriver` class, which implements this interface:

```php
<?
//class.mysqldriver.php
include("interface.dbdriver.php");
class MySQLDriver implements DBDriver
{


}
?>
```

Now if you execute the code above, it will give the following error because `MySQLDriver` class has no `connect()` and `execute()` function as defined in the interface. Let's run the code and read the error:

```
<b>Fatal error</b>: Class MySQLDriver contains 2 abstract methods
and must therefore be declared abstract or implement the remaining
methods (DBDriver::connect, DBDriver::execute) in <b>C:\OOP with
PHP5\Codes\ch1\class.mysqldriver.php</b> on line <b>5</b><br />
```

Well, now we have to add those two methods in our `MySQLDriver` class. Let's see the code below:

```php
<?
include("interface.dbdriver.php");
class MySQLDriver implements DBDriver
{
  public function connect()
  {
    //connect to database
  }
  public function execute()
  {
    //execute the query and output result
  }
}
?>
```

If we run the code now, we get the following error message again:

```
<b>Fatal error</b>:  Declaration of MySQLDriver::execute() must be
compatible with that of DBDriver::execute() in <b>C:\OOP with
PHP5\Codes\ch1\class.mysqldriver.php</b> on line <b>3</b><br />
```

The error message is saying that our `execute()` method is not compatible with the `execute()` method structure that was defined in the interface. If you now take a look at the interface, you will find that `execute()` method should have one argument. So that means whenever we implement an interface in our class, every method structure must exactly be the same as defined in the interface. Let's rewrite our `MySQLDriver` class as follows:

```
<?
include("interface.dbdriver.php");
class MySQLDriver implements DBDriver
{
  public function connect()
  {
    //connect to database
  }
  public function execute($query)
  {
    //execute the query and output result
  }
}
?>
```

Abstract Class

An abstract class is almost the same as interface, except that now the methods can contain body. An abstract class must also be "extended", not "implemented". So if the extended classes have some methods with common functionalities, then you can define those functions in an abstract class. Let's see the example below:

```
<?
//abstract.reportgenerator.php
abstract class ReportGenerator
{
  public function generateReport($resultArray)
  {
    //write code to process the multidimensional result array and
    //generate HTML Report
  }
}
?>
```

In our abstract class we have a method named `generateReport`, which takes a multidimensional array as argument and then generates an HTML report using it. Now, why did we put this method in an abstract class? Because generating a report will be a common function to all DB Drivers and it doesn't affect the code because it is taking only one array as an argument, not anything relevant to DB itself. Now we can use this abstract class in our `MySQLDriver` class as shown below. Please note that all the code to generate the report is already written, so we need not write code for that method in our driver class again as we did for interfaces.

```
<?
include("interface.dbdriver.php");
include("abstract.reportgenerator.php");
class MySQLDriver extends ReportGenerator implements DBDriver
{
  public function connect()
  {
    //connect to database
  }
  public function execute($query)
  {
    //execute the query and output result
  }
  // You need not declare or write the generateReport method here
  //again as it is extended from the abstract class directly."
}
?>
```

Please note that we can use the abstract class and implement an interface concurrently as shown in the above example.

> You cannot declare an abstract class as final, because abstract class means it has to be extended and final class means it can't be extended. So it's totally meaningless to use these two keywords together. PHP won't allow you to use them together.

Similar to declaring a class as abstract, you can also declare any method as abstract. When a method is declared as abstract, it means that the subclass must override that method. An abstract method should not contain any body where it is defined. An abstract method can be declared as shown here:

```
abstract public function connectDB();
```

Static Method and Properties

A `static` keyword is very important in object oriented programming. Static methods and properties play a vital role in application design and also in design patterns. So what are static methods and properties?

You have already seen that to access any method or attribute in a class you must create an instance (i.e. using `new` keyword, like `$object = new emailer()`), otherwise you can't access them. But there is a difference for static methods and properties. You can access a static method or property directly without creating any instance of that class. A static member is like a global member for that class and all instances of that class. Also, static properties persist the last state of what it was assigned, which is very useful in some cases.

You might ask why someone uses a static method. Well, most of the static methods are similar to utility methods. They perform a very specific task, or return a specific object (static properties and methods are used significantly in design patterns, we will learn that later). So declaring a new object every time for those works might be considered resource extensive. Let's see an example of static methods.

Consider that in our application we keep support for all three databases, MySQL, PostgreSQL, and SQLite. Now we need to use one particular driver at a time. For that, we are designing a `DBManager` class, which can instantiate any driver on demand and return that to us.

```
<?
//class.dbmanager.php
class DBManager
{
  public static function getMySQLDriver()
  {
    //instantiate a new MySQL Driver object and return
  }
  public static function getPostgreSQLDriver()
  {
    //instantiate a new PostgreSQL Driver object and return
  }
  public static function getSQLiteDriver()
  {
    //instantiate a new MySQL Driver object and return
  }
}
?>
```

How do we use this class? You can access any static property using a : : operator and not using the - > operator. Let's see the example below:

```
<?
//test.dbmanager.php
include_once("class.dbmanager.php");
$dbdriver = DBManager::getMySQLDriver();
//now process db operation with this $dbdriver object
?>
```

Notice that we didn't create any instance of DBManager object like $dbmanager = new DBManager(). Rather we directly access one of its methods using the : : operator.

So how does this benefit us? Well, we just need a driver object, so no need to create a new DBManager object and commit it to memory as long as our scripts are executing. Static methods usually perform a specific task and finish it.

Here are some important things to note. You can't use $this pseudo object inside a static method. As the class is not instantiated, $this doesn't exist inside a static method. You should rather use the self keyword.

Let's take a look at the following example. It shows how a static property actually works:

```
<?
//class.statictester.php
class StaticTester
{
  private static $id=0;
  function __construct()
  {
    self::$id +=1;
  }
  public static function checkIdFromStaticMehod()
  {
    echo "Current Id From Static Method is ".self::$id."\n";
  }
  public function checkIdFromNonStaticMethod()
  {
    echo "Current Id From Non Static Method is ".self::$id."\n";
  }
}
$st1 = new StaticTester();
StaticTester::checkIdFromStaticMehod();
```

```
$st2 = new StaticTester();
$st1->checkIdFromNonStaticMethod(); //returns the val of $id as 2
$st1->checkIdFromStaticMehod();
$st2->checkIdFromNonStaticMethod();
$st3 = new StaticTester();
StaticTester::checkIdFromStaticMehod();
?>
```

You will see the output is as follows:

```
Current Id From Static Method is 1
Current Id From Non Static Method is 2
Current Id From Static Method is 2
Current Id From Non Static Method is 2
Current Id From Static Method is 3
```

Whenever we create a new instance, it affects all the instances as the variable is declared as static. Using this special facility, a special design pattern "Singleton" works perfectly in PHP.

> **Caution: Using Static Members**
>
> Static members make object oriented much like old procedural programming; without creating instances, you can directly call any function, like the old days. That's why we use static method with caution. Excessive static methods make no use at all. Unless you have any specific purpose, don't use static members.

Accessor Methods

Accessor methods are simply methods that are solely devoted to get and set the value of any class properties. It's a good practice to access class properties using accessor methods instead of directly setting or getting their value. Though accessor methods are the same as other methods, there are some conventions writing them.

There are two types of accessor methods. One is called `getter`, whose purpose is returning value of any class property. The other is setter that sets a value into a class property. Let's see how to write the `getter` and `setter` methods for class properties:

```
<?
class Student
{
  private $name;
  private $roll;
```

```php
    public function setName($name)
    {
      $this->name= $name;
    }
    public function setRoll($roll)
    {
      $this->roll =$roll;
    }
    public function getName()
    {
      return $this->name;
    }
    public function getRoll()
    {
      return $this->roll;
    }
  }
  ?>
```

In the above example there are two `getter` methods and two `setter` methods. There is a convention in writing `accessor` methods. A `setter` method should start with `set` and the property name with the first character capitalized. A `getter` method should start with `get` followed by the variable name with the first letter capitalized. That means if we have a property named `email`, the getter method should be named as `getEmail` and the setter method should be named as `setEmail`. That's it.

So you might ask why someone does these extra jobs, when they can easily set these variables as public and leave everything else as is. Aren't all these the same? Well, no. Using accessor methods, you get some extra benefits. You will have full control while setting or retrieving the value of any property. "So what?" You might ask. Let's use a scenario where you need to filter users' input and set into properties. In this case, a `setter` can help you to filter the input before setting them into work.

Does this mean we have to write 100 `getter` and `setter` methods if my class contains 100 properties? You ask as good question. PHP is kind enough to relieve you from this boredom. How? Let us see the next section where we discuss using magic methods for setting and getting property values dynamically. Those methods will reduce the stress up to 90%. Don't you believe me? Let's see.

Using Magic Methods to Set/Get Class Properties

We discussed in the previous section that writing accessor method for a number of properties will be a real nightmare. To avoid that boredom, you can use magic methods. This process is called property overloading.

PHP5 introduced some magic methods in classes to reduce the pain of OOP in some cases. Two of those magic methods are introduced to set and get dynamic property values in a class. These two magic methods are named as __get() and __set(). Let us see how to use them:

```php
<?
//class.student.php
class Student
{
  private $properties = array();
  function __get($property)
  {
    return $this->properties[$property];
  }
  function __set($property, $value)
  {
    $this->properties[$property]="AutoSet {$property} as: ".$value;
  }
}
?>
```

Now let us see the code in action. Use the class above with the following script:

```php
<?
$st = new Student();
$st->name = "Afif";
$st->roll=16;
echo $st->name."\n";
echo $st->roll;
?>
```

When you execute the preceding code, PHP recognizes immediately that no property named name or roll exists in the class. Since the named property doesn't exist, the __set() method is called, which then assigns the value to the newly-created property of the class, allowing you to see the following output:

```
AutoSet name as: Afif
AutoSet roll as: 16
```

Seems quite interesting, huh? Using magic methods you still have full control over setting and retrieving property values in classes. However, you have one limitation if you use magic methods. While using reflection API, you can't investigate class properties (we will discuss about reflection API in a later chapter). Moreover, your class lost the "readability" and "maintainability" quite a lot. Why? See the code of previous `Student` class and new `Student` class and you will understand that for yourself.

Magic Methods for Overloading Class Methods

Like overloading, and using the accessor methods, there are magic methods to overload any method call in a class. If you are still not familiar with method overloading, then this is a process of accessing any method that doesn't even exist in the class. Sounds funny, right? Let's take a closer look.

There is a magic method, which helps to overload any method call in PHP5 class context. The name of that magic method is `__call()`. This allows you to provide actions or return values when undefined methods are called on an object. It can be used to simulate method overloading, or even to provide smooth error handling when an undefined method is called on an object. `__call` takes two arguments: the name of the method and an array of the arguments passed to the undefined method.

For example see the code below:

```
<?
class Overloader
{
  function __call($method, $arguments)
  {
    echo "You called a method named {$method} with the following
                                       arguments <br/>";
    print_r($arguments);
    echo "<br/>";
  }
}
$ol = new Overloader();
$ol->access(2,3,4);
$ol->notAnyMethod("boo");
?>
```

If you see the code above, then you will see that there is no method called `access` and `notAnyMethod`. So therefore, it should raise an error, right? However, the method overloader still helps you to call any non existing method. If you execute the code above, you will get the following output.

```
You called a method named access with the following arguments
Array
(
    [0] => 2
    [1] => 3
    [2] => 4
)
You called a method named notAnyMethod with the following arguments
Array
(
    [0] => boo
)
```

That means you will get all arguments as an array. There are many more magic methods, which you will learn step-by-step in this book.

Visually Representing a Class

In OOP, sometimes you have to visually represent your class. Let's learn how to visually represent a class. For this, we will use our `Emailer` class this time.

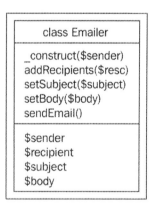

In this graphical representation, there are three sections. At the top most section a class name should be written. In the second section all methods with or without parameters are written. And in the third box all the properties are written. That's it!

Summary

In this chapter we have learned how to create objects and interact between them. PHP5 brings amazing improvements in object models when compared to PHP4. Zend Engine 2, which is at the core of PHP5, is also very efficient in handling these features with great performance optimization.

In the next chapter we will go through more details and the core features of OOP in PHP. But before starting next chapter, please practice everything discussed here, otherwise you may get confused in some topics. Practice them as much as you can, try to refactor all your previous code in OOP. The more you practice, the more efficient you become.

3
More OOP

The previous chapter creates a basis for us to kick-start OOP with PHP. This chapter will deal with some advanced features in more detail. For example, we will learn about class information functions by which we can investigate details about any class. We will then learn about some handy object-oriented information functions and also one of the great new features in PHP5, which is exception handling.

This chapter will also introduce us to the Iterators for easier array access. To store any object for later use, we need to use a special feature in OOP which is called serialization, we will also learn about this here. As a whole this chapter will strengthen your base in OOP.

Class Information Functions

If you want to investigate and gather more information regarding any class, these functions will be your light in the dark. These functions can retrieve almost any information regarding a class. But there is an improved version of these functions and is introduced as a totally new set of API in PHP5. That API is called **reflection**. We will learn about reflection API in Chapter 5.

Checking if a Class Already Exists

When you need to check if any class already exists in the current scope, you can use a function named `class_exists()`. Have a look at the following example:

```
<?
include_once("../ch2/class.emailer.php");
echo class_exists("Emailer");
//returns true otherwise false if doesn't exist
?>
```

The best way to use the `class_exists()` function is to first check if a class is already available. You can then create an instance of that class if it is available. This will make your code much more stable.

```
<?
include_once("../ch2/class.emailer.php");
if( class_exists("Emailer"))
{
  $emailer = new Emailer("hasin@pageflakes.com");
}
else
{
  die("A necessary class is not found");
}
?>
```

Finding Currently Loaded Classes

In some cases you may need to investigate which classes are loaded in the current scope. You can do it pretty fine with the `get_declared_classes()` function. This function will return an array with currently available classes.

```
<?
include_once("../ch2/class.emailer.php");
print_r(get_declared_classes());
?>
```

You will see a list of currently available classes on the screen.

Finding out if Methods and Properties Exists

To find out if a property and/or a method is available inside the class, you can use the `method_exists()` and `property_exists()` functions. Please note, these functions will return true only if the properties and methods are defined in public scope.

Checking the Type of Class

There is a function called `is_a()` that you can use to check the type of class. Take a look at the following example:

```
<?
class ParentClass
{
```

```
    }
class ChildClass extends ParentClass
{
}
$cc = new ChildClass();
if  (is_a($cc,"ChildClass")) echo "It's a ChildClass Type Object";
echo "\n";
if  (is_a($cc,"ParentClass")) echo "It's also a ParentClass Type
Object";
?>
```

You will find the output as follows:

```
Its a ChildClass Type Object
Its also a ParentClass Type Object
```

Finding Out the Class Name

In the previous example we checked the class if it's a type of a known one. What if
we need to get the original name of the class itself? No worry, we have the
get_class() function to help us.

```
<?
class ParentClass
{
}
class ChildClass extends ParentClass
{
}
$cc = new ChildClass();
echo get_class($cc)
?>
```

As an output, you should get ChildClass. Now take a look at the following
example, which "brjann" enlisted as unexpected behaviour in the PHP manual user
note section.

```
<?
class ParentClass
{
  public function getClass()
{
    echo get_class(); //using "no $this"
  }
}
class Child extends ParentClass
{
```

```
}
$obj = new Child();
$obj->getClass(); //outputs "ParentClass"
?>
```

If you run this code, you will see `ParentClass` as the output. But why? You are calling the method for a `Child`. Is it unexpected? Well, no. Take a serious look at the code. Though the `Child` extended the `ParentClass` object, it didn't override the method `getClass()`. So the method is still running under a `ParentClass` scope. That's why it returns the result `ParentClass`.

So what actually happened to the following piece of code? Why is it returning `Child`?

```
<?
class ParentClass {
  public function getClass(){
     echo get_class($this); //using "$this"
   }
}
class Child extends ParentClass {
}
$obj = new Child();
$obj->getClass(); //outputs "child"
?>
```

In the `ParentClass` object, the `get_class()` function returns `$this` object, which clearly holds a reference of `Child` class. That's why you are getting `Child` as your output.

Exception Handling

One of the most improved features in PHP5 is that you can now use exceptions, like other OOP languages out there. PHP5 introduces these exception objects to simplify your error management.

Let's see how these exceptions occur and how to handle them. Take a look at the following class, which simply connects to a PostgreSQL server. In the case of failing to connect to the server, let's see what it usually returns:

```
<?
//class.db.php
class db
{
   function connect()
   {
```

```
      pg_connect("somehost","username","password");
    }
}
$db = new db();
$db->connect();
?>
```

The output is the following.

```
<b>Warning</b>: pg_connect() [<a href='function.pg-connect'>
function.pg-connect</a>]: Unable to connect to PostgreSQL
server: could not translate host name "somehost" to address:
Unknown host in <b>C:\OOP with PHP5\Codes\ch3\exception1.php</b>
on line <b>6</b><br />
```

How are you going to handle it in PHP4? Generally, by using something similar to the following shown below:

```
<?
//class.db.php
error_reporting(E_ALL - E_WARNING);
class db
{
  function connect()
  {
    if (!pg_connect("somehost","username","password")) return false;
  }
}
$db = new db();
if (!$db->connect()) echo "Falied to connect to PostgreSQL Server";
?>
```

Now let's see how we can solve it with exception.

```
<?
//class.db.php
error_reporting(E_ALL - E_WARNING);
class db
{
  function connect()
  {
    if (!pg_connect("host=localhost password=pass user=username
                     dbname=db")) throw new Exception("Cannot connect
                     to the database");
  }
```

```
}
$db = new db();
try {
  $db->connect();
}
catch (Exception $e)
{
  print_r($e);
}
?>
```

The output will be something like this:

```
Exception Object
(
  [message:protected] => Cannot connect to the database
  [string:private] =>
  [code:protected] => 0
  [file:protected] => C:\OOP with PHP5\Codes\ch3\exception1.php
  [line:protected] => 8
  [trace:private] => Array
    (
      [0] => Array
        (
          [file] => C:\OOP with PHP5\Codes\ch3\exception1.php
          [line] => 14
          [function] => connect
          [class] => db
          [type] => ->
          [args] => Array
            (
            )
        )
      [1] => Array
        (
          [file] => C:\Program Files\Zend\ZendStudio-
                                5.2.0\bin\php5\dummy.php
          [line] => 1
          [args] => Array
            (
              [0] => C:\OOP with PHP5\Codes\ch3\exception1.php
            )
          [function] => include
        )
    )
)
```

So you get a lot of things in this exception class. You can catch all the errors using this try-catch block. You can use try-catch inside another try-catch block. Take a look at the following example. Here we developed two of our own exception objects to make the error handling more structured.

```php
<?
include_once("PGSQLConnectionException.class.php");
include_once("PGSQLQueryException.class.php");
error_reporting(0);
class DAL
{
  public $connection;
  public $result;
  public function connect($ConnectionString)
  {
    $this->connection = pg_connect($ConnectionString);
    if ($this->connection==false)
    {
      throw new PGSQLConnectionException($this->connection);
    }
  }
  public function execute($query)
  {
    $this->result = pg_query($this->connection,$query);
    if (!is_resource($this->result))
    {
      throw new PGSQLQueryException($this->connection);
    }
    //else do the necessary works
  }
}
$db = new DAL();
try{
  $db->connect("dbname=golpo user=postgres2");
  try{
    $db->execute("select * from abc");
  }
  catch (Exception $queryexception)
  {
    echo $queryexception->getMessage();
  }
}
catch(Exception $connectionexception)
{
  echo $connectionexception->getMessage();
}
?>
```

Now, if the code cannot connect to DB, it catches the error and displays that **Sorry, couldn't connect to PostgreSQL server**: message. If the connection is successful but the problem is in the query, it will display the proper information. If you check the code, then you will find that for a connection failure we throw a `PGSQLConnectionException` object, and for a query failure we just throw a `PGSQLQueryException` object. We can custom develop these objects by extending the core Exception class of PHP5. Let's take a look at the code. The first one is the `PGSQLConnectionException` class.

```
<?
Class PGSQLConnectionException extends Exception
{
  public function __construct()
  { $message = "Sorry, couldn't connect to postgresql server:";
    parent::__construct($message, 0000);
  }
}
?>
```

And here comes `PGSQLQueryException` class

```
<?
Class PGSQLQueryException extends Exception
{
  public function __construct($connection)
  {
    parent::__construct(pg_last_error($connection),0);
  }
}
?>
```

That's it!

Collecting all PHP Errors as Exception

If you want to collect all PHP errors (except the FATAL errors) as exception, you can use the following code:

```
<?php
function exceptions_error_handler($severity, $message,
      $filename, $lineno) {
         throw new ErrorException($message, 0, $severity,
         $filename, $lineno);
      }
set_error_handler('exceptions_error_handler');
?>
```

The credit of the above code piece goes to `fjoggen@gmail.com`, which I collected from the PHP manual user notes.

Iterators

An Iterator is a new command introduced in PHP5 to help traversing through any object. Check out the following example to understand what Iterators are actually used for. In PHP4 you could iterate through an array as shown in the following example, using `foreach` statement:

```
<?
foreach($anyarray as $key=>$val)
{
   //do something
}
?>
```

You could also perform a `foreach` operation over an object, let's take a look at the following example.

```
<?
class EmailValidator
{
   public $emails;
   public $validemails;
}
$ev = new EmailValidator();
foreach($ev as $key=>$val)
{
   echo $key."<br/>";
}
?>
```

This code will output the following:

```
emails
validemails
```

Please note that it can only iterate through the public properties. But what if we want just the valid email addresses as the output? Well, in PHP5 that's possible by implementing the `Iterator` and `IteratorAggregator` interface. Let us see using the following example. In this example, we create a `QueryIterator`, which can iterate through a valid PostgreSQL query result and returns one row per Iteration.

```
<?
class QueryIterator implements Iterator
{
   private $result;
```

```
      private $connection;
      private $data;
      private $key=0;
      private $valid;
      function __construct($dbname, $user, $password)
      {
        $this->connection = pg_connect("dbname={$dbname} user={$user}");
      }
      public function exceute($query)
      {
        $this->result = pg_query($this->connection,$query);
         if (pg_num_rows($this->result)>0)
        $this->next();
      }
      public function rewind() {}
      public function current() {
        return $this->data;
      }
      public function key() {
        return $this->key;
      }
      public function next() {
        if ($this->data = pg_fetch_assoc($this->result))
        {
          $this->valid = true;
          $this->key+=1;
        }
        else
        $this->valid = false;
      }
      public function valid() {
        return $this->valid;
      }
    }
    ?>
```

Let's see the code in action.

```
    <?
    $qi= new QueryIterator("golpo","postgres2","");
    $qi->exceute("select name, email from users");
    while ($qi->valid())
    {
```

```
    print_r($qi->current());
    $qi->next();
}
?>
```

For example, if there are two records in our table `users`, you will get the following output:

```
Array
(
    [name] => Afif
    [email] => mayflower@phpxperts.net
)
Array
(
    [name] => Ayesha
    [email] => florence@phpxperts.net
)
```

Quite handy, don't you think?

ArrayObject

Another useful object introduced in PHP5 is `ArrayObject` that wraps the regular PHP array and gives it an OO flavor. You can programmatically access the array in an OO style. You can create an `ArrayObject` object by simply passing to `ArrayObject` constructor. `ArrayObject` has the following useful methods:

append()

This method can add any value at the end of the collection.

getIterator()

This method simply creates an `Iterator` object and return so that you can perform iteration using an Iterator style. This is a very useful method for getting an `Iterator` object from any array.

offsetExists()

This method can determine whether the specified offset exists in the collection.

offsetGet()

This method returns the value for specified offset.

offsetSet()

Like `offsetGet()`, this method can set any value to the specified `index()`.

offsetUnset()

This method can unset the element at specified index.

Let us see some examples of `ArrayObject`:

```
<?
$users = new ArrayObject(array("hasin"=>"hasin@pageflakes.com",
    "afif"=>"mayflower@phpxperts.net",
    "ayesha"=>"florence@pageflakes.net"));
$iterator = $users->getIterator();
while ($iterator->valid())
{
  echo "{$iterator->key()}'s Email address is
        {$iterator->current()}\n";
        $iterator->next();
}
?>
```

Array to Object

We can access any array element by its key, for example `$array[$key]`. However, what if we want to access it like this, `$array->key` style? It's very easy and we can do it by extending `ArrayObject`. Let's see using the following example.

```
<?
class ArrayToObject extends ArrayObject
{
  public function __get($key)
  {
    return $this[$key];
  }
  public function __set($key,$val)
  {
    $this[$key] = $val;
  }
}
?>
```

Now let's see it in action:

```
<?
$users = new ArrayToObject(array("hasin"=>"hasin@pageflakes.com",
    "afif"=>"mayflower@phpxperts.net",
```

```
        "ayesha"=>"florence@pageflakes.net"));
    echo $users->afif;
    ?>
```

It will output the email address associated with the key `afif`, as follows:

```
    mayflower@phpxperts.net
```

This example may come in handy if you want to convert the array of any known format into an object.

Accessing Objects in Array Style

In the previous section we learned how to access any array in OO style. What if we want to access any object in array style? Well, PHP provides that facility too. All you have to do is implement `ArrayAccess` interface in your class.

`ArrayAccess` interface has four methods, which you must implement in the class. The methods are `offsetExists()`, `offsetGet()`, `offsetSet()`, `offsetUnset()`. Let's create a sample class implementing `ArrayAccess` interface.

```php
<?php
class users implements ArrayAccess
{
  private $users;
    public function __construct()
{
        $this->users = array();
    }
    public function offsetExists($key)
{
        return isset($this->users[$key]);
    }
    public function offsetGet($key)
{
        return $this->users[$key];
    }
    public function offsetSet($key, $value)
{
        $this->users[$key] = $value;
    }
    public function offsetUnset($key)
{
        unset($this->users[$key]);
    }
```

```
}
$users = new users();
$users['afif']="mayflower@phpxperts.net";
$users['hasin']="hasin@pageflakes.com";
$users['ayesha']="florence@phpxperts.net";
echo $users['afif']
?>
```

The output will be mayflower@phpxperts.net.

Serialization

So far we have learned how we can create objects and manipulate them. Now what happens if you need to save any state of the object and retrieve it later exactly in that form? In PHP, you can achieve this functionality by serialization.

Serialization is a process of persisting the state of an object in any location, either physical files or in variables. To retrieve the state of that object, another process is used which is called "unserialization". You can serialize any object using serialize() function. Let's see how we can serialize an object:

```
<?
class SampleObject
{
  public $var1;
  private $var2;
  protected $var3;
  static $var4;

  public function __construct()
  {
    $this->var1 = "Value One";
    $this->var2 = "Value Two";
    $this->var3 = "Value Three";
    SampleObject::$var4 = "Value Four";
  }
}
$so = new SampleObject();
$serializedso =serialize($so);
file_put_contents("text.txt",$serializedso);
echo $serializedso;
?>
```

The script will output a string, which PHP understands how to unserialize.

Now it's time to retrieve our serialized object and convert into a usable PHP object. Please bear in mind that the class file you are unserializng must be loaded first.

```
<?
include_once("class.sampleobject.php");
$serializedcontent = file_get_contents("text.txt");
$unserializedcontent = unserialize($serializedcontent);
print_r($unserializedcontent);
?>
```

What do you think the output will be? Take a look:

```
SampleObject Object
(
   [var1] => Value One
   [var2:private] => Value Two
   [var3:protected] => Value Three
)
```

It's now a regular PHP object; the same as it was just before serializing. Please note that all variables keep their values, which were set before serializing, except the static one. You cannot save the state of a static variable by serializing.

What if we didn't include the class file by `include_once` before unserializing? Let's just comment out the first line, which includes the class file and then run the example code. You will get the following output:

```
__PHP_Incomplete_Class Object
(
   [__PHP_Incomplete_Class_Name] => SampleObject
   [var1] => Value One
   [var2:private] => Value Two
   [var3:protected] => Value Three
)
```

At this point, you can't use it as the object again.

Magic Methods in Serialization

Do you remember we overloaded properties and methods using some magic methods like __get, __set, and __call? For serialization, you are allowed to use some magic methods to hook into the process of serialization. PHP5 provides two magic methods for this purpose named __sleep and __awake. These methods give some control over the whole process.

Let's develop all the static variables of a process using these magic methods, which we generally won't be able to do without a hack. Normally it's not possible to serialize the values of any static variables and return the object in same state with that static variable. However, we can make it happen, let's see the following code.

```php
<?
class SampleObject
{
  public $var1;
  private $var2;
  protected $var3;
  public static $var4;

  private $staticvars = array();

  public function __construct()
  {
    $this->var1 = "Value One";
    $this->var2 = "Value Two";
    $this->var3 = "Value Three";
    SampleObject::$var4 = "Value Four";
  }
  public function __sleep()
  {
    $vars = get_class_vars(get_class($this));
    foreach($vars as $key=>$val)
    {
      if (!empty($val))
      $this->staticvars[$key]=$val;
    }
    return array_keys( get_object_vars( $this ) );
  }
  public function __wakeup()
  {
    foreach ($this->staticvars as $key=>$val){
      $prop = new ReflectionProperty(get_class($this), $key);
      $prop->setValue(get_class($this), $val);
    }
    $this->staticvars=array();
  }
}
?>
```

What happens if we serialize the object, write it into the file and then later retrieve the state? You will find the static value still persists the last value assigned to it.

Let's discuss the code for a second. The __sleep function performs all the necessary operations. It searches for public properties with values and stores the variable's name when it finds one into a private variable staticvars. Later when someone tries to unserialize the object, it retrieves each value from the staticvars and writes it to the property itself. Pretty handy, don't you agree?

You will notice that we haven't used a hack, with the exception of the theoretical capability of the __sleep() and __wakeup() functions. So what are these two functions useful for? Where can we use them in practice? This is actually fairly simple. For example, if your class has any resource object associated with it (a live DB connection, a reference of an open file) in sleep function you can properly close them as they are no longer usable when someone unserializes it. Please remember that in an unserialized state someone may still use those resource pointers. So in the __wakeup() function you can open those DB connections, or file pointers, to give it an exact shape as it was before. Let us see using the following example:

```php
<?
class ResourceObject
{
  private $resource;
  private $dsn;
  public function __construct($dsn)
  {
    $this->dsn = $dsn;
    $this->resource = pg_connect($this->dsn);
  }
  public function __sleep()
  {
    pg_close($this->resource);
    return array_keys( get_object_vars( $this ) );
  }
  public function __wakeup()
  {
    $this->resource = pg_connect($this->dsn);
  }
}
?>
```

This object, when being serialized, will free the memory that was consumed by $resource. Later, when it will be unserialized, it will open the connection again using the DSN string. So now, after unserialization, everything is as it was before. That's the clue!

Object Cloning

PHP5 introduces a new approach while copying objects from one into another, which is quite different to PHP4. In PHP4 when you copy an object to another, it performs a deep copy. This means it just makes a completely new object, which retains the properties of the object being copied. However, changing anything in the new object will not affect the main object.

PHP5 is different from this in the way it makes a shallow copy when you copy an object from one to another. To clearly understand the situation, you need to understand the following code.

```
<?
$sample1 = new StdClass();
$sample1->name = "Hasin";
$sample2 = $sample1;
$sample2->name = "Afif";
echo $sample1->name;
?>
```

If you run the above code in PHP5 can you guess what will you get as the result? Hasin or Afif? Surprisingly, the output is Afif. As I mentioned earlier, PHP5 performs a shallow copy while copying an object; $sample2 is just a reference to $sample1. So whenever you perform any change to $sample1 object or $sample2 object, it will affect both.

In PHP4 it works differently; it will output Hasin, as both are different from each other.

If you want to perform the same in PHP5, you have to use the clone keyword. Let's take a look at the following example

```
<?
$sample1 = new stdClass();
$sample1->name = "Hasin";
$sample2 =clone $sample1;
$sample2->name = "Afif";
echo $sample1->name;
?>
```

The output now would be Hasin.

Autoloading Classes or Classes on Demand

While working with big projects, another very good practice is loading classes only when you need it. That means you shouldn't over consume the memory by loading unnecessary classes all the time.

In our examples, you have seen that we include the original class file before making them available in our script. Unless you include the class file, you can't create an instance of it. PHP5 introduces a feature to auto load your class files so that you don't have to bother to include them manually. Usually, this feature is helpful in big applications where you have to deal with lots of classes and don't want to bother to call `include` all the time. Take a look at the following example:

```php
<?
function __autoload($class)
{
    include_once("class.{$class}.php");
}
$s = new Emailer("hasin@somewherein.net");
?>
```

When you execute the script shown above, note that we didn't include any class file for the `Emailer` class. Because of this `__autoload()` function, PHP5 will auto load a file named `class.emailer.php` in the current directory. So you need not worry about including the class yourself.

Method Chaining

Method chaining is another process introduced in PHP5 by which you can directly access the methods and attributes of an object when it is returned by any function. It is something like the following:

```php
$SomeObject->getObjectOne()->getObjectTwo()->callMethodOfObjectTwo();
```

The above code means that `$someObject` class has a method named `getObjectOne()` which returns an object named `$objectOne`. This `$objectOne` has another method named `getObjectTwo()` which returns an object whose method is called by the final call.

So who is going to use such things? Let's take a look at the following code; it makes you understand beautifully how a method chain can be used in real life:

```php
$dbManager->select("id","email")->from("user")->where("id=1")
                                ->limit(1)->result();
```

Do you find the above code meaningful and readable? The code returns a row from the user table containing the ID and email where the value of ID is equal to 1. Have you ever wondered how to design such a DB manager object? Let's take a look at this great example below:

```
<?
class DBManager
{
  private $selectables = array();
  private $table;
  private $whereClause;
  private $limit;
  public function select()
  {
    $this->selectables=func_get_args();
    return $this;
  }
  public function from($table)
  {
    $this->table = $table;
    return $this;
  }
  public function where($clause)
  {
    $this->whereClause = $clause;
    return $this;
  }
  public function limit($limit)
  {
    $this->limit = $limit;
    return $this;
  }
  public function result()
  {
    $query = "SELECT ".join(",",$this->selectables)." FROM
                                      {$this->table}";
    if (!empty($this->whereClause))
    $query .= " WHERE {$this->whereClause}";
    if (!empty($this->limit))
    $query .= " LIMIT {$this->limit}";
    echo "The generated Query is : \n".$query;
  }
}
$db= new DBManager();
$db->select("id","name")->from("users")->where("id=1")->
                                      limit(1)->result();
?>
```

The output is:

```
The generated Query is :
SELECT id,name FROM users WHERE id=1 LIMIT 1
```

The class automatically builds the query. So how does this work? Well, in PHP5 you can return objects; so using this feature we return the object on each method that we want to be part of the chain. Now, it's just a matter of a few minutes to execute that query and return the result. Surprising, you can also execute the following code which generates the same result:

```
$db->from("users")->select("id","name")->limit(1)->where("id=1")
                                                   ->result();
```

This is the beauty of PHP5; it's amazingly powerful.

Life Cycle of an Object in PHP and Object Caching

If you are interested in understanding the lifecycle of an object, then an object is live until the script ends. As soon as the script finishes executing, any object instantiated by this script also dies. Unlike web tier in Java, there is no global or application-level scope in PHP. So you cannot persist the object normally. If you want to persist an object, you can serialize it and later unserialize it when necessary. Manually handling this serialization and unserialization process may seem boring sometimes. It would really be nice to store the object somewhere and retrieve it later (well, the same as serialization/unserialization process, but with more flexibly).

There is some object caching technology available for PHP, which is very efficient indeed. The most successful among them is **memcached**. PHP has an extension to memcached API, which is available to download from PECL. Memcached runs as a standalone server and caches objects directly into memory. Memcached server listens in a port. PHP memcached API understands how to talk to the memcached server, hence it saves and retrieves an object with its help. In this section we will demonstrate how to work with memcached, but we will not go into too much detail.

You can download the memcached server from `http://danga.com/memcached`. If you are using Linux you have to compile it by your own. With some distro you will find the memcached package. You will find a `win32` binary version of memcached 1.2.1 server from `http://jehiah.cz/projects/memcached-win32/` which is developed by kronuz (`kronuz@users.sourceforge.net`). After getting the executable, give the following command in the console. It will start the memcached server.

```
memcached -d install
```

This will install memcached as a service.

```
memcached -d start
```

This will start the daemon/service.

Now it's time to store some objects into the memcached server and retrieve it.

```
<?
$memcache = new Memcache;
$memcache->connect('localhost', 11211) or die ("Could not connect");
$tmp_object = new stdClass;
$tmp_object->str_attr = 'test';
$tmp_object->int_attr = 12364;
$memcache->set('obj', $tmp_object, false, 60*5) or die ("Failed to
save data at the server");
?>
```

When you execute the code above, the memcache server saves the object $tmp_object against the key obj for five minutes. After five minutes this object will not exist. By this time, if you need to restore that object, you can execute the following code:

```
<?
$memcache = new Memcache;
$memcache->connect('localhost', 11211) or die ("Could not connect");
$newobj = $memcache->get('obj');
?>
```

That's it. Memcache is so popular that it has Perl, Python, Ruby, Java, and Dot Net, and C port.

Summary

In this chapter we learned how to use some advanced OOP concepts in PHP. We learned how to retrieve information from any object, and learned about ArrayAccess, ArrayObject, Iterators, and some other native objects which simplifies the life of a developer. Another very important thing we learned from this chapter is Exception Handling.

In next chapter we will learn about design patterns and how to use them in PHP. Untill then, happy exploring…

4
Design Patterns

Object oriented programming was basically introduced to ease the development process as well as reduce the time of development by reducing amounts of code. If properly planned and designed, OOP can increase the performance of the program to a great extent. One of those magical performance cum code reduction issues is "Design Pattern" which was introduced by Eric Gamma and his three other friends in the book *Design Patterns* in 1972. Because of four authors, the book was introduced as written by *Gang of Four* or simply *Goff*. In that legendary book, Gang of Four introduced several patterns to minimize the amount of code as well as to introduce effective coding practice. In this chapter we will learn some of those patterns to implement in PHP.

You Might have Done this Before…

While coding, many of us use these patterns without being aware that these techniques are actually known as patterns. Even in my early coding life, I used some coding techniques, which I later found out to be similar to some patterns. So don't be afraid about using patterns. They are daily coding tricks, which you may have always performed, but you may not have known.

While developing software, some problems are addressed on a regular basis. Almost every software development faces some of these problems. These problems are termed "design patterns" and are given some common solutions. So knowing design patterns saves a lot of time for developers in software development. Let's have a closer look at design patterns.

Strategy Pattern

One of the common problems we face whilst programming, is that we have to make decisions on different strategies. Strategy pattern is a common pattern helps us make decisions on different cases, more easily. To understand this better, let us use a scenario that you're developing a notifier program. This notifier program will check the given options for a user. A user may want to be notified in many ways, like email, SMS, or fax. Your program has to check the available options to contact that user and then make a decision upon that. This case can easily be solved by Strategy pattern:

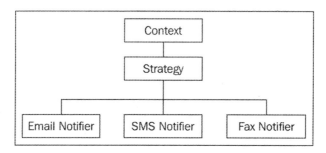

In the above pattern we are using three classes called SMSNotifier, EmailNotifier, and FaxNotifier. All these classes implement the Notifier interface, which has a method named notify. Each of these classes implement that method on their own.

Let's create the interface first.

```
<?
//interface.Notifier.php
interface notifier
{
   public function notify();
}
?>
```

Now we will create different types of notifiers.

```
class.emailnotifier.php
<?
include_once("interface.notifier.php");
class EmailNotifier implements notifier
{
   public function notify()
   {
      //do something to notify the user by Email
   }
}
?>
```

`class.faxnotifier.php`

```php
<?
include_once("notifier.php");
class FaxNotifier implements notifier
{
  public function notify()
  {
    //do something to notify the user by Fax
  }
}
?>
```

`class.smsnotifier.php`

```php
<?
include_once("notifier.php");
class SMSNotifier implements notifier
{
  public function notify()
  {
    //do something to notify the user by SMS
  }
}
?>
```

Now we will use this code:

```php
<?
include_once("EmailNotifier.php");
include_once("FaxNotifier.php");
include_once("SMSNotifier.php");
/**
 * Let's create a mock object User which we assume has a method named
 * getNotifier(). This method returns either "sms" or "fax" or "email"
 */
$user = new User();
$notifier = $user->getNotifier();
switch ($notifier)
{
  case "email":
    $objNotifier = new EmailNotifier();
    break;
  case "sms":
    $objNotifier = new SMSNotifier();
    break;
  case "fax":
    $objNotifier = new FaxNotifier();
```

```
      break;
  }
  $objNotifier->notify();
  ?>
```

I'm sure you'll agree that this is pretty simple. I am also sure that you have already used such solutions in your existing codes on more than one occasion

Factory Pattern

Another common design pattern is factory pattern. The main goal of this pattern is delivering an object by hiding all the complexities behind it. This may sound cryptic, so let's look at it using a real life scenario.

You are doing a project that works on a very complex system. For this example, you are creating an online document repository, which saves documents in temporary storage. For this you need support for PostgreSQL, MySQL, Oracle, and SQLite because users may deploy your application using any of these. So you create an object, which connects to MySQL and perform the necessary tasks. Your MySQL object is:

```
<?
class MySQLManager
{
  public function setHost($host)
  {
    //set db host
  }
  public function setDB($db)
  {
    //set db name
  }
  public function setUserName($user)
  {
    //set user name
  }
  public function setPassword($pwd)
  {
    //set password
  }
  public function connect()
  {
    //now connect
  }
}
?>
```

Well, now you use this class like this:

```
<?
$MM = new MySQLManager();
$MM->setHost("host");
$MM->setDB("db");
$MM->setUserName("user");
$MM->setPassword("pwd");
$MM->connect();
?>
```

You can now see that before you started using your class, you needed to do a lot of things. Your PostgreSQL class also looks similar:

```
<?
class PostgreSQLManager
{
  public function setHost($host)
  {
    //set db host
  }
  public function setDB($db)
  {
    //set db name
  }
  public function setUserName($user)
  {
    //set user name
  }
  public function setPassword($pwd)
  {
    //set password
  }
  public function connect()
  {
    //now connect
  }
}
?>
```

And usage is also the same:

```
<?
$PM = new PostgreSQLManager();
$PM->setHost("host");
$PM->setDB("db");
```

```
$PM->setUserName("user");
$PM->setPassword("pwd");
$PM->connect();
?>
```

But now usage could be a bit difficult when you merge them together:

```
<?
  If ($dbtype=="mysql")
  //use mysql class
  Else if ($dbtype=="postgresql")
  //use postgresql class
?>
```

Shortly after this you will find that as more database engines are added, the core code changes significantly and you have to hard code all these things in core classes. However, a very good practice of programming is loose coupling. Here you make a separate class called DBManager, which will perform all these things from a central place. Let's make it:

```
<?
class DBManager
{
  public static function setDriver($driver)
  {
    $this->driver = $driver;
  //set the driver
  }
  public static function connect()
  {
    if ($this->driver=="mysql")
    {
      $MM = new MySQLManager();
      $MM->setHost("host");
      $MM->setDB("db");
      $MM->setUserName("user");
      $MM->setPassword("pwd");
      $this->connection = $MM->connect();
    }
    else if($this->driver=="pgsql")
    {
      $PM = new PostgreSQLManager();
      $PM->setHost("host");
      $PM->setDB("db");
      $PM->setUserName("user");
```

```
        $PM->setPassword("pwd");
        $this->connection= $PM->connect();
      }
    }
  }
?>
```

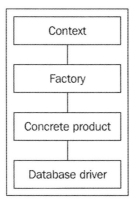

Now you can use it from a single place called DBManager. This makes the thing a whole lot easier than before.

```
<?
$DM = new DBManager();
$DM->setDriver("mysql");
$DM->connect("host","user","db","pwd");
?>
```

This is the real life example of a Factory design pattern. The DBManager now works as a Factory, which encapsulates all the complexities behind the scene and delivers two products. Factory simplifies programming by encapsulating the difficulties inside it.

Abstract Factory

Abstract Factory is almost similar to Factory, the only difference is that all your concrete objects must extend a common abstract class. You may ask what is the benefit of doing so is. Well, as long as concrete objects are derived from a known abstract object, programming is simplified because they all come in the same standard.

Let's have a look at the previous example. We first create an abstract class and then extend that object to develop all concrete driver classes.

```php
<?
abstract class DBDriver
{
  public function connect();
  public function executeQuery();
  public function insert_id();
  public function setHost($host)
  {
    //set db host
  }
  public function setDB($db)
  {
    //set db name
  }
  public function setUserName($user)
  {
    //set user name
  }
  public function setPassword($pwd)
  {
    //set password
  }
  //.....
}
?>
```

Now our MySQL will be derived from it:

```php
<?
class MySQLManager extends DBDriver
{
  public function connect()
  {
    //implement own connection procedures
  }
  public function executeQuery()
  {
    //execute mysql query and return result
  }
  public function insertId()
  {
    //find the latest inserted id
  }
}
?>
```

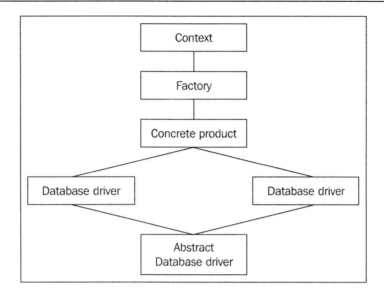

Later we will use this `MySQLManager` class as usual in our `DBManager`. One major benefit is that we define all the necessary functions in a single place, which is present in all derived classes with the same standard. We can also encapsulate common functions/procedures in the abstract class.

Adapter Pattern

Another interesting problem in OOP is solved by a design pattern named Adapter. So what is an Adapter pattern and what type of problems does it solve?

Adapter is actually an object that acts like an adapter in real life, in that it converts one thing to another. Using Adapter you can convert electric sources from higher to lower volts. Similarly in OOP, using Adapter pattern, one object can fit for the same methods of another object.

Let us discuss patterns in real life coding in more detail. Suppose you develop an online document repository, which exports written documents to popular online file storage services. You have developed one wrapper, which can store and retrieve documents from Writely using their native API. Well, soon after Google acquired Writely, you find that they are temporarily shut down and you have to use Google docs as the base of that repository. Now what will you do? You find open source solutions to use with Google docs but unfortunately you find that the methods of that Google doc object differ from the Writely object.

This is a very common scenario and it happens when classes are developed by different developers. You want to use this Google docs object but you don't want to change your core code, because then you will have to change it a lot then. On top of this there are chances that the code may break after these core changes.

In this scenario an Adapter pattern comes to save your life. You develop a common interface which a Writely object implements. Now all you have to do is develop another wrapper class, which implements the same interface that was implemented by Google Docs. So what will our wrapper class do? It wraps all the methods of Google docs class into those available in the interface. After successfully wrapping everything, you can use this object straight in your code. You may need to change a line or two, but the rest of the core code remains unchanged.

That's what's great about using Adapter pattern. You can keep your core code unchanged even when the code of third-party dependencies and external API changes. Let us have a closer look at it:

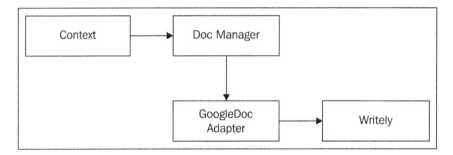

Here comes our first version of a Writely object:

```
<?
class Writely implements DocManager()
{
  public function authenticate($user, $pwd)
  {
    //authenticate using Writely authentication scheme
  }
  public function getDocuments($folderid)
  {
    //get documents available in a folder
  }
  public function getDocumentsByType($folderid, $type)
  {
    //get documents of specific type from a folder
  }
```

```
    public function getFolders($folderid=null)
    {
      //get all folders under a specific folder
    }
    public function saveDocuments($document)
    {
      //save the document
    }
  }
  ?>
```

Here is the DocManager interface:

```
  <?
  interface DocManager
  {
    public function authenticate($user, $pwd);
    public function getDocuments($folderid);
    public function getDocumentsByType($folderid, $type);
    public function getFolders($folderid=null);
    public function saveDocument($document);
  }
  ?>
```

Now the GoogleDoc object looks like something below:

```
  <?
  class GoogleDocs
  {
    public function authenticateByClientLogin()
    {
      //authenticate using Writely authentication scheme
    }
    public function setUser()
    {
      //set user
    }
    public function setPassword()
    {
      //set password
    }
    public function getAllDocuments()
    {
      //get documents available in a folder
    }
```

```
    public function getRecentDocuments()
    {

    }
    public function getDocument()
    {
    }
  }
?>
```

So how does it fit with our existing code?

To make it compatible with our existing code, we need to develop the wrapper object, which implements the same DocManager interface but uses the GoogleDoc object to perform the actual work.

```
<?php
Class GoogleDocsAdapter implements DocManager
{
  private $GD;
  public function __construct()
  {
    $this->GD = new GoogleDocs();
  }
  public function authenticate($user, $pwd)
  {
    $this->GD->setUser($user);
    $this->GD->setPwd($pwd);
    $this->GD->authenticateByClientLogin();
  }
  public function getDocuments($folderid)
  {
    return $this->GD->getAllDocuments();
  }
  public function getDocumentsByType($folderid, $type)
  {
    //get documents using GoogleDocs object and return only
    // which match the type
  }
  public function getFolders($folderid=null)
  {
    //for example there is no folder in GoogleDocs, so
    //return anything.
```

```
    }
    public function saveDocument($document)
    {
      //save the document using GoogleDocs object
    }
  }
  ?>
```

Now we will just instantiate an instance of `GoogleDocsAdapter` and then use that instance in our core code. As it implements the same interface, there is no need to change the core code.

However, there's one more thing to note: what about the missing functions? For example your `WritelyDocs` object supports the `getFolders()` method, which is of no use in `GoogleDocs`. You must implement those methods more carefully. For example, if your core code requires some folder ID returned by this method, in `GoogleDocsAdapter` you can generate a random folder ID and return them (which has no use in `GoogleDocsAdapter`). So your core code won't break at all.

Singleton Pattern

One of the most used design patterns is Singleton. This pattern solves a very significant problem in object oriented programming and saves the lives of millions of programmers in practical programming.

The main purpose of the Singleton pattern is to deliver a single instance of object no matter how many times you instantiate it. That is, if an object is instantiated once, using the Singleton pattern you can deliver only that instance when you require it again in your code. This saves memory consumption by preventing the creation of multiple instances of an object. Thus Singleton pattern is used to improve the performance of your application.

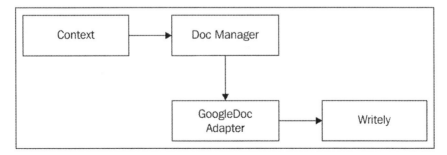

Let's take the `MySQLManager` class, which we created in the previous example. Now we are adding a single instance feature using Singleton pattern.

```php
<?
class MySQLManager
{
  private static $instance;

  public function __construct()
  {
    if (!self::$instance)
    {
      self::$instance = $this;
      echo "New Instance\n";
      return self::$instance;
    }
    else
    {
      echo "Old Instance\n";
      return self::$instance;
    }
  }
//keep other methods same
}
?>
```

Now let us see how it actually works. If you execute the following script, you will be surprised to see the result.

```php
<?
$a = new MYSQLManager();
$b = new MYSQLManager();
$c = new MYSQLManager();
$d = new MYSQLManager();
$e = new MYSQLManager();
?>
```

The output is:

```
New Instance
Old Instance
Old Instance
Old Instance
Old Instance
```

Strange, isn't it? The MySQLManager class creates only a single instance at the very first call, after that it is using the same old object instead of creating a new object all the time. Let us see how we achieve it.

```
private static $instance;
```

Our class has a static variable named $instance. At the constructor we check if the static variable actually contains anything. If it is empty, we instantiate the object itself and set the instance in this static variable. As it is static, it will remain available throughout the execution of this script.

Let us get back to the constructor. At the second call, we just check if the $instance variable contains anything. We find that the $instance variable is actually containing an instance of this object, and it is still preserved because it is a static variable. So in the second call, we actually return the instance of this object, which was created by the previous call.

Singleton is a very important pattern and you should understand properly what it actually does. You can optimize your application and increase its performance using this pattern properly.

Iterator Pattern

Iterator is a common pattern, which helps you to manipulate a collection more easily. Almost every language has built-in support of Iterators. Even PHP5 has a built-in Iterator objects. Iterators are very useful to provide an easy interface to manipulate a collection sequentially.

Let us consider this scenario when the Iterator pattern can save the life if a developer is in complex applications. Let us imagine you are creating a blog, where users write their daily web logs. How can you display the different posts, one by one?

In the following example you pass all the post_id made by an author in your template and the template designer writes the following code to display it properly in the template:

```
<?
$posts = getAllPosts(); //example function return all post ids of this
author
for($i = 0; $i<count($posts); $i++)
{
  $title = getPostTitle($post[$i]);
  echo $title;
  $author = getPostAuthor($post[$i]);
```

```
$content = parseBBCode(getPostContent($post[$i]));
echo "Content";
$comments = getAllComments($post[$i]);
for ($j=0; $j<count($comments); $j++)
{
  $commentAuthor = getCommentAuthor($comments[$j]);
  echo $commentAuthor;
  $comment = getCommentContent($comments[$j]);
  echo $comment;
}
}
?>
```

In this example we do everything in the template; we fetch all post ids, then get authors, comments, content, and display it. We also fetch the comments list in the template code. The whole code is too hazy to read and manage and may crash successively at any core changes. But just think, if we turn the comments into a collection of comment object for that post and all the posts into a collection of post object for easier accessing, it will remove the burden of template designing as well as create manageable code.

Let us implement Iterator pattern for our comments and posts and see how effectively it turns your code into a readable piece of poem. After all, coding is poetry.

To use iteration effectively in PHP5 we can use `Iterator` interface. The interface is shown below:

```
<?
interface Iterator
{
  function rewind();
  function current();
  function key();
  function next();
  function valid();
}
?>
```

The `rewind()` function of Iterator sets the index to the start of collection. The `Current()` returns the current object. `key()` function returns the current key. The Function `next()` returns if there are more object ahead in the current loop counter. If the return is yes, this function returns true, otherwise it returns false. The `valid()` function returns the current object if it has any value in it. Let us create an Iterator for our post object.

We will create a function named `getAllPosts()` that will return all posts from the DB. All these posts are returned as a `Post` object, which has methods like `getAuthor()`, `getTitle()`, `getDate()`, `getComments()`, etc. Now we will create the Iterator:

```php
<?php
class Posts implements Iterator
{
  private $posts = array();
  public function __construct($posts)
  {
    if (is_array($posts)) {
      $this->posts = $posts;
    }
  }
  public function rewind() {
    reset($this->posts);
  }
  public function current() {
    return current($this->posts);
  }
  public function key() {
    return key($this->var);
  }
  public function next() {
    return next($this->var);
  }
  public function valid() {
    return ($this->current() !== false);
  }
}
?>
```

Now let's use the Iterator we just created.

```php
<?
$blogposts = getAllPosts();
$posts = new Posts($posts);
foreach ($posts as $post)
{
  echo $post->getTitle();
  echo $post->getAuthor();
  echo $post->getDate();
  echo $post->getContent();
  $comments = new Comments($post->getComments());
  //another Iterator for comments, code is same as Posts
```

```
    foreach ($comments as $comment)
    {
      echo $comment->getAuthor();
      echo $comment->getContent();
    }
  }
  ?>
```

The code becomes much readable and maintainable now.

 In PHP array, object implements this Iterator interface by default. But of course you can implement it to add many more user-defined functionalities to ease your development cycle.

Observer Pattern

You might wonder how these events actually work and how they are raised. Well, if you are familiar with the Observer pattern, you can create event driven applications easier than ever.

An Observer pattern solves a common problem in OOP. For example, if you want some objects to be notified automatically when something happens (an event raised), you can solve that problem with this pattern. Let us take a closer look.

An Observer pattern consists of two types of objects; one is an observable object, which is observed by `observer` object. When the state of an observable object changes, it notifies all observers registered with it.

So where can it be used? Actually it is being used everywhere. Think about a logging application, which can log errors in different ways when an error occurs. Think about a messenger application, which pops up when the latest message arrives. Think about a web bulletin board where the latest messages display automatically whenever a new message is posted. Well, there are thousands more. Let us implement this pattern.

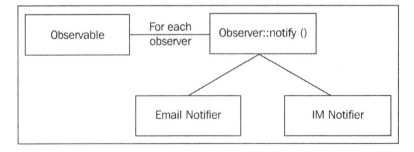

ement `observer` interface as shown below:

```
();
```

which we will notify when the state of an observable

```
ments observer
```

```
fy()
```

```
g YM
ι YM\n";
```

```
ments observer
```

```
()
```

```
ʔmail
ʔmail\n";
```

ver.

```
();
object)
```

```
bserver )
ect;
```

```
plement observer interface\n";
```

```
    public function stateChange()
    {
      foreach ($this->observers as $observer)
      {
        $observer->notify();
      }
    }
  }
  ?>
```

Now let us use it:

```
<?
$postmonitor = new observable();
$ym = new YMNotifier();
$em = new EmailNotifier();
$s= new stdClass();
$postmonitor->register($ym);
$postmonitor->register($em);
$postmonitor->register($s);
$postmonitor->stateChange();
?>
```

The output is as follows:

```
The object must implement observer interface
Notifying via YM
Notifying via Email
```

Proxy Pattern or Lazy Loading

Another very important programming practice in OOP is lazy loading and loose coupling. The main idea is to decrease the concrete dependency among objects while coding. What is the benefit of such programming? One simple answer — it always increases the portability of your code.

Using the Proxy pattern you can create a local version of a remote object. It provides a common API for accessing methods of a remote object without knowing the things behind the scene. The best example of a Proxy pattern could be the XML RPC and SOAP client and server for PHP.

Let's take a look at the following code. Here we are creating a class, which can access any method of a remotely created object. The methods of a remote object are exposed via the XML RPC server and then they are accessed via XML RPC clients.

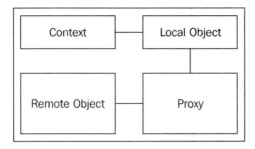

If you are wondering how it works, you will find that almost every blog engine supports three popular blogging API: i.e. Blogger, MetaWebLog, and MovableType. Using these methods you can remotely manage your blog. Which methods are supported, will depend on the blog engine.

We will use Incutio PHP XML-RPC library to create a sample server and client object. Let us create a server first. You can download the XML-RPC Library from here: `http://scripts.incutio.com/xmlrpc/IXR_Library.inc.php.txt`

We are creating a time server from which we can get Greenwich Mean Time (GMT):

```php
<?php
include('IXR_Library.inc.php');
function gmtTime() {
    return gmdate("F, d Y H:i:s");
}
$server = new IXR_Server(array(
    'time.getGMTTime' => 'gmtTime',
));
?>
```

Well very simple. We just create some methods and then map them to the XML RPC server. Now let us see how we can code for clients:

```php
<?
include('IXR_Library.inc.php');
$client = new IXR_Client('http://localhost/proxy/server.php');
if (!$client->query('time.getGMTTime'))
{
    die('Something went wrong - '.$client->getErrorCode().' :
                                   '.$client->getErrorMessage());
}
echo ($client->getResponse());
?>
```

If you place the server in your web server (here `localhost`) document, the root in a folder named `proxy` and then access the client, you will get the following output:

March, 28 2007 16:13:20

That's it! This is how Proxy pattern works and gives interface to remote objects for local applications.

Decorator Pattern

Decorator pattern is an important problem-solving approach introduced by GoF in their legendary design pattern book. Using this pattern you can add additional functionalities in an existing object without extending an object. So you might ask what is the benefit of adding additional functionalities without inheritance.

Well, there certainly are some benefits. To extend an object, sometimes you need to know many inner things of that class. Sometimes it's not possible to extend the class without rewriting the existing functionalities. If you want to add the same functionalities to many types of objects, it is much better to add them using Decorator pattern instead of extending all of them individually. Otherwise it might lead you to a horrible maintenance nightmare.

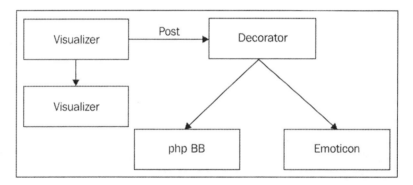

Let us go for a common scenario. For example, imagine that you are building a blog or message board where all your posts and comments come as separate post and comment objects. Both of these objects have a common method `getContents()` which returns the filtered content of that post or comment.

Now your manager is asking to add functionalities to parse emoticon and BBCode of those posts and comments. The core code is complex and you don't want to touch it anymore. Here Decorator pattern comes to save your life.

Let us see our Post and Comment object first.

```php
<?
class Post
{
  private $title;
  private $content;
  //additional properties
  public function filter()
  {
    //do necessary processing
    $this->content = $filtered_content;
    $this->title = $filtered_title;
  }
  public function getContent()
  {
    return $this->content;
  }
  //additional methods
}
?>
<?
class Comment
{
  private $date;
  private $content;
  //additional properties
  public function filter()
  {
    //do necessary processing
    $this->content = $filtered_content;
  }
  public function getContent()
  {
    return $this->content;
  }
  //additional methods
}
?>
```

Now we create two Decorator objects, which can parse the BBCode and Emoticon respectively:

```
<?
class BBCodeParser
{
  private $post;
  public function __construct($object)
  {
    $this->post = $object;
  }
  public function getContent()
  {
    //parse bbcode
$post->filter();
    $content = $this->parseBBCode($post->getContent());
    return $content;
  }
  private function parseBBCode($content)
  {
    //process BB code in the content and return it
  }
}
?>
```

And here comes the emoticon parser:

```
<?
class EmoticonParser
{
  private $post;
  public function __construct($object)
  {
    $this->post = $object;
  }
  public function getContent()
  {
    //parse bbcode
    $post->filter();
    $content = $this->parseEmoticon($post->getContent());
    return $content;
  }
  private function parseEmoticon($content)
  {
```

```
        //process Emoticon code in the content and return it
    }
  }
?>
```

These Decorator objects just add the BBCode and EmoticonCode parsing capability to the existing objects without touching them.

Let us see how we can use that:

```
<?
$post = new Post();//set the properties of the post object
$comment = new Comment();//set the properties of the comment object
$post->filter();
$comment->filter();
if ($BBCodeEnabled==false && $EmoticonEnabled==false)
{
  $PostContent = $post->getContent();
  $CommentContent = $comment->getContent();
}
elseif ($BBCodeEnabled==true && $EmoticonEnabled==false)
{
  $bb = new BBCodeParser($post);//passing a post object to
                               //BBCodeParser
  $PostContent = $bb->getContent();
  $bb = new BBCodeParser($comment);//passing a comment object to
                                   //BBCodeParser
  $CommentContent = $bb->getContent();
}
elseif ($BBCodeEnabled==true && $EmoticonEnabled==false)
{
  $em = new EmoticonParser($post);
  $PostContent = $bb->getContent();

  $em = new EmoticonParser($comment);
  $CommentContent = $bb->getContent();
}
?>
```

This is how you can add additional functionalities to existing objects without even touching them. However, you saw that BBCodeParser and EmoticonParser accept any object, which means that if you supply an object, which doesn't have any method named getContent(), the code will crash. So you can implement a common interface in those objects, which you might want to decorate. Also in the Decorator object you can accept only those objects, which implement that or those interfaces.

Active Record Pattern

This is another very important design pattern to simplify database manipulation. We will learn more about this pattern in Chapter 7.

Facade Pattern

So far we have learned many common problem-solving approaches using design patterns in OOP. Here comes another interesting pattern, which we often use unintentionally in our code without knowing that it is also a pattern. Let us learn about this common pattern named Facade pattern.

Facade provides a common interface to many objects. In other words, it just simplifies the programming providing a necessary interface, which actually uses a lot of other objects behind the scenes. Thus it minimizes the learning curve for developers. When a new developer joins the team, he suddenly gets introduced to a lot of objects with tons of methods and properties, among which he might need a few to accomplish his work. So why bother spending time learning them all? This is where Facade helps developers and saves a lot of their time. Let's look at some examples to understand it more clearly.

Suppose you are creating an apartment rental system, where you have three objects in your repository. One object performs the geocoding with the help of online geocoding services. Another object locates that place using a map service. Finally, another service searches all the apartments for sale in that area.

Now you want to create an easier interface over these three so that any future developer can work with your library instead of studying them all together. The following picture shows us the code structure before there is a Facade:

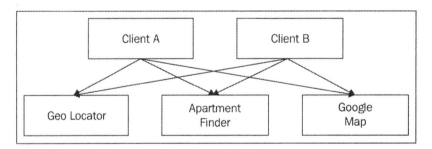

Here is the code structure after using Facade:

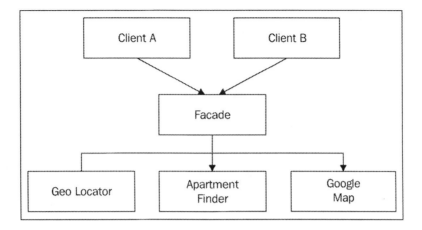

Now let us take a look at the code:

```php
<?
class ApartmentFinder
{
  public function locateApartments($place)
  {
    //use the web service and locate all apartments suitable
    //search name
    //now return them all in an array
    return $apartmentsArray();
  }
}
?>
<?
class GeoLocator
{
  public function getLocations($place)
  {
    //use public geo coding service like yahoo and get the
    //lattitude and
    //longitude of that place
    return array("lat"=>$lattitude, "lng"=>$longitude);
  }
}
?>
<?
class GoogleMap
{
```

```
    public function initialize()
    {
      //do initialize
    }
    public function drawLocations($locations /* array */)
    {
      //locate all the points using Google Map Locator
    }
    public function dispatch($divid)
    {
      //draw the map with in a div with the div id
    }
  }
  ?>
```

These are our concrete classes. Now you want to develop a Facade using all of them and provide an easier interface for developers. See how easy it makes combining three of them:

```
  <?
  class Facade
  {
    public function findApartments($place, $divid)
    {
      $AF = new ApartmentFinder();
      $GL =new GeoLocator();
      $GM = new GoogleMap();
      $apartments = $AF->locateApartments($place);
      foreach ($apartments as $apartment)
      {
        $locations[] = $GL->getLocations($apartment);
      }
      $GM->initialize();
      $GM->drawLocations($locations);
      $GM->dispatch($divid);
    }
  }
  ?>
```

Anyone can now use the service of all three classes using only one single interface Facade:

```
<?
$F = new Facade();
$F->findApartments("London, Greater London","mapdiv");
?>
```

As I said before, in object oriented programming we have done this type of job several times in our times in our project, however we might not have known that the technique is defined as a design pattern named Facade.

Summary

Design patterns are an essential part of OOP. It makes your code more effective, better performing, and easier to maintain. Sometimes we implement these design patterns in our code without knowing that these solutions are defined as design patterns. There are many design patterns as well, which we cannot cover in this book, because it would then simply be a book on just design patterns. However, if you are interested in learning other design patterns, you can read *Head First Design Patterns* published by O'reilly and *Design Patterns Explained* by Addison-Wesley.

Don't think that you have to implement design pattern in your code. Use them only when you need them. Proper usage of correct patterns can make your code perform better; similarly using them improperly could make your code slow and less efficient.

In the next chapter we will learn about another important section of OOP in PHP. That is Unit testing and Reflections. Until then, keep playing with the patterns and explore them.

5
Reflection and Unit Testing

PHP5 brings in many new flavors compared to PHP4. It replaces many old APIs with smarter, new ones. One of them is Reflection API. Using this cool set of API, you can reverse engineer any class or object to figure out its properties and methods. You can invoke those methods dynamically and do some more. In this chapter we will learn in more detail about reflections and use of each of these functions.

Another very important part of software development is building test suits for automated testing of your piece of work. This is to ensure it's working correctly and after any changes it maintains backward compatibility. To ease the process for PHP developers, there are a lot of testing tools available on the market. Among them are some very popular tools like PHPUnit. In this chapter we will learn about unit testing with PHP.

Reflection

Reflection API provides some functionality to find out what is inside an object or a class at runtime. Besides that, reflection API lets you invoke dynamically any method or property of any object. Let's get our hands dirty with reflection. There are numerous objects introduced in reflection API. Among them, the following are important:

```
class Reflection { }
interface Reflector { }
class ReflectionException extends Exception { }
class ReflectionFunction implements Reflector { }
class ReflectionParameter implements Reflector { }
class ReflectionMethod extends ReflectionFunction { }
class ReflectionClass implements Reflector { }
class ReflectionObject extends ReflectionClass { }
class ReflectionProperty implements Reflector { }
class ReflectionExtension implements Reflector { }
```

Let us go and play with `ReflectionClass` first.

ReflectionClass

This is one of the major core classes in reflection API. This class helps you to reverse engineer any object in the broad sense. The structure of this class is shown here:

```php
<?php
class ReflectionClass implements Reflector
{
    final private __clone()
    public object __construct(string name)
    public string __toString()
    public static string export(mixed class, bool return)
    public string getName()
    public bool isInternal()
    public bool isUserDefined()
    public bool isInstantiable()
    public bool hasConstant(string name)
    public bool hasMethod(string name)
    public bool hasProperty(string name)
    public string getFileName()
    public int getStartLine()
    public int getEndLine()
    public string getDocComment()
    public ReflectionMethod getConstructor()
    public ReflectionMethod getMethod(string name)
    public ReflectionMethod[] getMethods()
    public ReflectionProperty getProperty(string name)
    public ReflectionProperty[] getProperties()
    public array getConstants()
    public mixed getConstant(string name)
    public ReflectionClass[] getInterfaces()
    public bool isInterface()
    public bool isAbstract()
    public bool isFinal()
    public int getModifiers()
    public bool isInstance(stdclass object)
    public stdclass newInstance(mixed args)
    public stdclass newInstanceArgs(array args)
    public ReflectionClass getParentClass()
    public bool isSubclassOf(ReflectionClass class)
    public array getStaticProperties()
    public mixed getStaticPropertyValue(string name [, mixed default])
```

```
:yValue(string name, mixed value)
:rties()

Eace(string name)
getExtension()
ame()
```

Unit Testing (handwritten)

rks. First we will find their methods

iternal structure of any object, which is almost

: internal name of an object, hence the

ie class is a built-in object inside PHP5.

ite of `isInternal()` method. It just returns
/ the user.

is the PHP script file name where the class

iich line the code of that class begins in the

iteresting function which returns the class
We will demonstrate it in examples later in

: reference of the constructor of the object as a

the address of any method passed to it as a
`ReflectionMethod` object.

/ of all the methods in the object. In that array
:flectionMethod object.

ns a reference to any property in that object, as

ray of constants in that object.

lue of any particular constant.

nterfaces that a class implemented (if any), you
ction which, returns an array of interfaces as

- The `getModifiers()` method returns the list of modifiers relevant to that class. For example, it could be public, private, protected, abstract, static, or final.
- `newInstance()` function returns a new instance of that class and returns it as a regular object (which is actually `stdClas`; `stdClass` is the base class of every PHP object).
- You want a reference to the parent class of any class? You can use `getParentClass()` method to get that as a `ReflectionClass` object.
- Another cool function of `ReflectionClass()` is that it can tell from which extension a class has been originated. For example, `ArrayObject` class is originated from SPL class. You have to use `getExtensionName()` function for that.

Let's write some code now. We will see these functions in real life code. Here, I am showing a fantastic example taken from the PHP Manual.

```php
<?php
interface NSerializable
{
    // ...
}
class Object
{
    // ...
}
/**
 * A counter class
 */
class Counter extends Object implements NSerializable
{
    const START = 0;
    private static $c = Counter::START;
    /**
     * Invoke counter
     *
     * @access  public
     * @return  int
     */
    public function count()
    {
        return self::$c++;
    }
}
// Create an instance of the ReflectionClass class
```

```php
$class = new ReflectionClass('Counter');
// Print out basic information
printf(
    "===> The %s%s%s %s '%s' [extends %s]\n" .
    "        declared in %s\n" .
    "        lines %d to %d\n" .
    "        having the modifiers %d [%s]\n",
        $class->isInternal() ? 'internal' : 'user-defined',
        $class->isAbstract() ? ' abstract' : '',
        $class->isFinal() ? ' final' : '',
        $class->isInterface() ? 'interface' : 'class',
        $class->getName(),
        var_export($class->getParentClass(), 1),
        $class->getFileName(),
        $class->getStartLine(),
        $class->getEndline(),
        $class->getModifiers(),
        implode(' ', Reflection::getModifierNames(
                                $class->getModifiers())))
        );
// Print documentation comment
printf("---> Documentation:\n %s\n",
                    var_export($class->getDocComment(), 1));
// Print which interfaces are implemented by this class
printf("---> Implements:\n %s\n",
                    var_export($class->getInterfaces(), 1));
// Print class constants
printf("---> Constants: %s\n",
                    var_export($class->getConstants(), 1));
// Print class properties
printf("---> Properties: %s\n",
                    var_export($class->getProperties(), 1));
// Print class methods
printf("---> Methods: %s\n",
                    var_export($class->getMethods(), 1));
// If this class is instantiable, create an instance
if ($class->isInstantiable())
{
    $counter = $class->newInstance();
    echo '---> $counter is instance? ';
    echo $class->isInstance($counter) ? 'yes' : 'no';
    echo "\n---> new Object() is instance? ";
    echo $class->isInstance(new Object()) ? 'yes' : 'no';
}
?>
```

Now save the above code in a file named `class.counter.php`. When you run the above code, you will get the following output:

X-Powered-By: PHP/5.1.1

Content-type: text/html

===> The user-defined class 'Counter' [extends ReflectionClass::__set_state(array(

  'name' => 'Object',

))]

    declared in PHPDocument2

    lines 15 to 29

    having the modifiers 0 []

---> Documentation:

'/**

* A counter class

*/'

---> Implements:

array (

  0 =>

  ReflectionClass::__set_state(array(

    'name' => 'NSerializable',

  )),

)

---> Constants: array (

  'START' => 0,

)

---> Properties: array (

  0 =>

ReflectionProperty::__set_state(array(

   'name' => 'c',

   'class' => 'Counter',

 )),

)

---> Methods: array (

 0 =>

 ReflectionMethod::__set_state(array(

   'name' => 'count',

   'class' => 'Counter',

 )),

)

---> $counter is instance? yes

---> new Object() is instance? No

ReflectionMethod

This is the class used to investigate any method of the class and then invoke it. Let us see the structure of this class:

```php
<?php
class ReflectionMethod extends ReflectionFunction
{
    public __construct(mixed class, string name)
    public string __toString()
    public static string export(mixed class, string name, bool return)
    public mixed invoke(stdclass object, mixed args)
    public mixed invokeArgs(stdclass object, array args)
    public bool isFinal()
    public bool isAbstract()
    public bool isPublic()
    public bool isPrivate()
    public bool isProtected()
    public bool isStatic()
```

```php
      public bool isConstructor()
      public bool isDestructor()
      public int getModifiers()
      public ReflectionClass getDeclaringClass()

      // Inherited from ReflectionFunction
      final private __clone()
      public string getName()
      public bool isInternal()
      public bool isUserDefined()
      public string getFileName()
      public int getStartLine()
      public int getEndLine()
      public string getDocComment()
      public array getStaticVariables()
      public bool returnsReference()
      public ReflectionParameter[] getParameters()
      public int getNumberOfParameters()
      public int getNumberOfRequiredParameters()
  }
  ?>
```

The most important methods of this class are getNumberOfParamaters, getNumberOfRequiredParameters, getParameters, and invoke. The first three of these are self explanatory; let's look at the fourth one which is invoked. This is a nice example taken from the PHP Manual:

```php
<?php
class Counter
{
    private static $c = 0;
    /**
     * Increment counter
     *
     * @final
     * @static
     * @access   public
     * @return   int
     */
    final public static function increment()
    {
        return ++self::$c;
    }
}
```

```
// Create an instance of the Reflection_Method class
$method = new ReflectionMethod('Counter', 'increment');
// Print out basic information
printf(
    "===> The %s%s%s%s%s%s%s%s method '%s' (which is %s)\n" .
    "      declared in %s\n" .
    "      lines %d to %d\n" .
    "      having the modifiers %d[%s]\n",
        $method->isInternal() ? 'internal' : 'user-defined',
        $method->isAbstract() ? ' abstract' : '',
        $method->isFinal() ? ' final' : '',
        $method->isPublic() ? ' public' : '',
        $method->isPrivate() ? ' private' : '',
        $method->isProtected() ? ' protected' : '',
        $method->isStatic() ? ' static' : '',
        $method->getName(),
        $method->isConstructor() ? 'the constructor' :
                                    'a regular method',
        $method->getFileName(),
        $method->getStartLine(),
        $method->getEndline(),
        $method->getModifiers(),
        implode(' ', Reflection::getModifierNames(
                            $method->getModifiers())))
        );
// Print documentation comment
printf("---> Documentation:\n %s\n",
                var_export($method->getDocComment(), 1));
// Print static variables if existant
if ($statics= $method->getStaticVariables()) {
    printf("---> Static variables: %s\n", var_export($statics, 1));
}
// Invoke the method
printf("---> Invokation results in: ");
var_dump($method->invoke(NULL));
?>
```

When executed, this code will give the following output:

```
===> The user-defined final public static method 'increment' (which is
a regular method)
      declared in PHPDocument1
      lines 14 to 17
      having the modifiers 261[final public static]
```

```
---> Documentation:
'/**
   * Increment counter
   *
   * @final
   * @static
   * @access  public
   * @return  int
   */'
---> Invokation results in: int(1)
```

ReflectionParameter

Another very important object in the reflection family is `ReflectionParameter`. Using this class you can analyze parameters of any method and take action accordingly. Let us take a look at the object structure:

```php
<?php
class ReflectionParameter implements Reflector
{
    final private __clone()
    public object __construct(string name)
    public string __toString()
    public static string export(mixed function, mixed parameter,
                                               bool return)
    public string getName()
    public bool isPassedByReference()
    public ReflectionFunction getDeclaringFunction()
    public ReflectionClass getDeclaringClass()
    public ReflectionClass getClass()
    public bool isArray()
    public bool allowsNull()
    public bool isPassedByReference()
    public bool getPosition()
    public bool isOptional()
    public bool isDefaultValueAvailable()
    public mixed getDefaultValue()
}
?>
```

To make things easier, have a look at the following example to see how this thing works.

```php
<?php
function foo($a, $b, $c) { }
function bar(Exception $a, &$b, $c) { }
function baz(ReflectionFunction $a,  $b = 1, $c = null) { }
function abc() { }
// Create an instance of Reflection_Function with the
// parameter given from the command line.
$reflect = new ReflectionFunction("baz");
echo $reflect;
foreach ($reflect->getParameters() as $i => $param)
{
    printf(
        "-- Parameter #%d: %s {\n".
        "   Class: %s\n".
        "   Allows NULL: %s\n".
        "   Passed to by reference: %s\n".
        "   Is optional?: %s\n".
        "}\n",
        $i,
        $param->getName(),
        var_export($param->getClass(), 1),
        var_export($param->allowsNull(), 1),
        var_export($param->isPassedByReference(), 1),
        $param->isOptional() ? 'yes' : 'no'
    );
}
?>
```

If you run the above code snippet, you will get the following output:

```
Function [ <user> <visibility error> function baz ]
{
  @@ C:\OOP with PHP5\Codes\ch5\test.php 4 - 4
  - Parameters [3]
  {
    Parameter #0 [ <required> ReflectionFunction &$a ]
    Parameter #1 [ <optional> $b = 1 ]
    Parameter #2 [ <optional> $c = NULL ]
  }
}
-- Parameter #0: a
{
   Class: ReflectionClass::__set_state(array(
   'name' => 'ReflectionFunction',
))
   Allows NULL: false
```

```
      Passed to by reference: true
      Is optional?: no
}
-- Parameter #1: b
{
      Class: NULL
      Allows NULL: true
      Passed to by reference: false
      Is optional?: yes
}
-- Parameter #2: c
{
      Class: NULL
      Allows NULL: true
      Passed to by reference: false
      Is optional?: yes
}
```

ReflectionProperty

This is the last one under the reflection family that we are going to discuss here. This class helps you to investigate class properties and reverse engineer them. This class has the following structure:

```php
<?php
class ReflectionProperty implements Reflector
{
    final private __clone()
    public __construct(mixed class, string name)
    public string __toString()
    public static string export(mixed class, string name, bool return)
    public string getName()
    public bool isPublic()
    public bool isPrivate()
    public bool isProtected()
    public bool isStatic()
    public bool isDefault()
    public int getModifiers()
    public mixed getValue(stdclass object)
    public void setValue(stdclass object, mixed value)
    public ReflectionClass getDeclaringClass()
    public string getDocComment()
}
?>
```

Here is an example taken directly from the PHP Manual, that helps describe how it actually works.

```php
<?php
class String
{
    public $length  = 5;
}
// Create an instance of the ReflectionProperty class
$prop = new ReflectionProperty('String', 'length');
// Print out basic information
printf(
    "===> The%s%s%s%s property '%s' (which was %s)\n" .
    "      having the modifiers %s\n",
        $prop->isPublic() ? ' public' : '',
        $prop->isPrivate() ? ' private' : '',
        $prop->isProtected() ? ' protected' : '',
        $prop->isStatic() ? ' static' : '',
        $prop->getName(),
        $prop->isDefault() ? 'declared at compile-time' :
                                    'created at run-time',
        var_export(Reflection::getModifierNames(
                                    $prop->getModifiers()), 1)
        );
// Create an instance of String
$obj= new String();
// Get current value
printf("---> Value is: ");
var_dump($prop->getValue($obj));
// Change value
$prop->setValue($obj, 10);
printf("---> Setting value to 10, new value is: ");
var_dump($prop->getValue($obj));
// Dump object
var_dump($obj);
?>
```

The code produces the following output upon execution. This code inspects a property with the help of ReflectionProperty and displays the following output:

```
===> The public property 'length' (which was declared at compile-time)
      having the modifiers array (
  0 => 'public',
)
```

```
---> Value is: int(5)
---> Setting value to 10, new value is: int(10)
object(String)#2 (1) {
  ["length"]=>
  int(10)
}
```

We will see some more uses of Reflection API in later chapters, when we will learn build an MVC framework.

Unit Testing

Another very important part of programming is unit testing, by which you can test pieces of code, whether it works perfectly or not. You can write test cases against any version of your code to check if your code works after refactoring. Unit testing ensures the workability of the code and helps to pin-point the problem when it occurs. When you code your application, unit tests works as your skeleton. Unit testing is a mandatory part of programming for programmers of every language. There are unit testing packages available for almost all major programming languages.

As with every other programming language, there is one package for Java that is considered as a standard model for every other unit testing package for other languages. This package is called as **JUnit** which is for Java developers. The standard and testing style maintained in JUnit is usually followed in many other unit testing packages. So JUnit has become a defacto in the unit testing area. The port of JUnit for PHP developers is known as **PHPUnit**, which was developed by Sebastian Bergmann. PHPUnit is a very popular unit testing package.

One of the main reasons for writing unit tests is that you cannot figure out all the bugs if you just write your code and deploy your application. There might be small bugs that might crash your application violently by returning a non relevant value. Don't overlook these small scenarios. There might be cases when you wouldn't imagine one of your codes returning an extremely odd result. Unit testing helps you by writing different test cases. Unit testing is not a thing which needs a lot of time to write, however the outcome is amazing.

In the following section we will learn the basics of unit testing, and get our hands dirty writing successful unit tests.

Benefits of Unit Testing

Unit testing has a lot of benefits, some of them are that it:

- Ensures the consistency of your application.
- Ensures the workability of your complete application after any kind of refactoring.
- Checks the redundancy and removes them from your code.
- Designs good API.
- Easily figures out where the problem is.
- Speeds up the debugging process if anything goes wrong; as you know particularly where the bug resides.
- Minimizes the effort of documentation by providing working examples of your API.
- Helps to do a regression test so that no regression occurs again.

A small Introduction to Vulnerable Bugs

Bugs can be of different types. Some bugs could just bother your users, some bug stops the functionality, and some bug vulnerability corrupts your resources. Let us consider the following example. You have written a function which takes two parameters and updates the database accordingly. The first parameter is the name of the field and the second parameter is the value of that field by which it should locate the data and then update them. Now let us design it:

```php
function selectUser($field, $condition)
{
  if (!empty($condition))
  {
    $query = "{$field}= '{$condition}'";
  }
  else
      $query = "{$field}";
      echo "select * from users where {$query}";
  $result = mysql_query("select * from users where {$query}");
  $results = array();
  while ($data = mysql_fetch_array($result))
  {
    $results[] = $data;
  }
  return $results;
}
```

Now when you call it like this, it shows a specific data:

```
print_r(selectUser("id","1");
```

The output is:

```
(
    [0] => Array
        (
            [0] => 1
            [id] => 1
            [1] => afif
            [name] => afif
            [2] => 47bce5c74f589f4867dbd57e9ca9f808
            [pass] => 47bce5c74f589f4867dbd57e9ca9f808
        )
)
```

But when you call it like this:

```
print_r(selectUser("id",$_SESSION['id']);
```

It displays the following:

```
(
    [0] => Array
        (
            [0] => 1
            [id] => 1
            [1] => afif
            [name] => afif
            [2] => 47bce5c74f589f4867dbd57e9ca9f808
            [pass] => 47bce5c74f589f4867dbd57e9ca9f808
        )
    1] => Array
        (
            [0] => 2
            [id] => 2
            [1] => 4b8ed057e4f0960d8413e37060d4c175
            [name] => 4b8ed057e4f0960d8413e37060d4c175
            [2] => 74b87337454200d4d33f80c4663dc5e5
            [pass] => 74b87337454200d4d33f80c4663dc5e5
        )
)
```

This is not a correct output; and as it is happening in runtime if it was update instead of a select query, your whole data may get corrupt. So how can you ensure that the output is always a valid one? Well, we will do that easily with unit testing later in this chapter.

Preparing for Unit Testing

To write successful unit test for PHP applications using PHPUnit, you need to download the package, configure it, and then do some small tasks before actually being able to execute your tests.

You can either run PHPUnit tests from the command line or from inside your script. For now we will run our tests from within our script, but in later sections, we will learn how to run unit tests from command line.

To start, download the package from `http://www.phpunit.de` and extract it in your include path. If you are not sure what is your include path you can get that from `include_path` settings in your `php.ini`. Or you can execute the following PHP script to display the output:

```
<?
echo get_include_path()
?>
```

Now extract the PHPUnit archive and place the PHPUnit folder in a folder, which is in your include path. This PHPUnit folder contains two other folders named `PHPUnit` and `PHPUnit2`.

You are done as soon as you place the folders in your include path directories. Now we are ready to go.

Starting Unit Testing

A unit test is actually a collection of different tests against your code. It is not a big job to write unit tests using PHPUnit. All you have to do is simply follow a set of conventions. Let's take a look at the following example, where you create a string manipulator class, which returns the number of words available in a string.

```
<?
//class.wordcount.php
class wordcount
{
  public function countWords($sentence)
  {
    return count(split(" ",$sentence));
  }
}
?>
```

Now we will write a unit test for this class. We have to extend the `PHPUnit_Framework_TestCase` to write any unit test. And we have to use `PHPUnit_Framework_TestSuite` to create the test suite, which actually holds a collection of tests. Then we will use `PHPUnit_TextUI_TestRunner` to run the tests from the suite and print the result.

```php
<?
//class.testwordcount.php
require_once "PHPUnit/Framework/TestCase.php";
require_once "class.wordcount.php";

class TestWordCount extends PHPUnit_Framework_TestCase
{
  public function testCountWords()
  {
    $Wc = new WordCount();
    $TestSentence = "my name is afif";
    $WordCount = $Wc->countWords($TestSentence);
    $this->assertEquals(4,$WordCount);
  }
}
?>
```

Running the test:

```php
<?
//testsuite.wordcount.php
require_once 'PHPUnit/TextUI/TestRunner.php';
require_once "PHPUnit/Framework/TestSuite.php";
require_once "class.testwordcount.php";

$suite = new PHPUnit_Framework_TestSuite();
$suite->addTestSuite("TestWordCount");
PHPUnit_TextUI_TestRunner::run($suite);
?>
```

Now if you run the code in `testsuite.wordcount.php` you will get the following output:

```
PHPUnit 3.0.5 by Sebastian Bergmann.
Time: 00:00
OK (1 test)
```

That means our test has passed and our word-counter function works perfectly, however, we will write some more test cases for that function.

Let us add this new test case in our `class.testwordcount.php`:

```
public function testCountWordsWithSpaces()
{
  $wc= new WordCount();
  $testSentence = "my name is Anonymous ";
  $wordCount = $Wc->countWords($testSentence);
  $this->assertEquals(4,$wordCount);
}
```

Now if we run our test suite we will get the following result:

```
PHPUnit 3.0.5 by Sebastian Bergmann.
.F
Time: 00:00
There was 1 failure:
1) testCountWordsWithSpaces(TestWordCount)
Failed asserting that <integer:5> is equal to <integer:4>.
C:\OOP with PHP5\Codes\ch5\UnitTest\FirstTest.php:34
C:\OOP with PHP5\Codes\ch5\UnitTest\FirstTest.php:40
C:\Program Files\Zend\ZendStudio-5.2.0\bin\php5\dummy.php:1
FAILURES!
Tests: 2, Failures: 1.
```

Here, we found that our foolproof word-count function fails. So what was our test input? We just add more spaces in our test parameter my name is afif, and then our function fails. This is because it splits the sentence with white space and returns the number of split parts. As there are more white spaces, so our function fails gracefully. That's a pretty nice test case; we found that our function might fail in real life if we release our code with this version of word counter. PHPUnit has become useful for us already. Now we will solve our function so that it returns the correct result if our sentence contains more white spaces. We change our `class.wordcount.php` to this new one:

```
class WordCount
{
  public function countWords($sentence)
  {
    $newsentence = preg_replace("~\s+~"," ",$sentence);
    return count(split(" ",$newsentence));
  }
}
```

Now if we run our test suite, it will give the following output.

```
PHPUnit 3.0.5 by Sebastian Bergmann.

..
Time: 00:00
OK (2 tests)
```

However we want more proof that our function will work better in the wild. So we are writing another test case. Let's add this new test case in our class.testwordcount.php:

```
public function testCountWordsWithNewLine()
{
  $Wc = new WordCount();
  $TestSentence = "my name is \n\r Anonymous";
  $WordCount = $Wc->countWords($TestSentence);
  $this->assertEquals(4,$WordCount);
}
```

And let's run the suit again. What is the result now?

```
PHPUnit 3.0.5 by Sebastian Bergmann.

...
Time: 00:00
OK (3 tests)
```

That's pretty satisfying. All our tests are running ok. The function is now a good one.

This is how unit test can help us in real life.

Testing an Email Validator Object

Now, let's repeat the steps again. This time we will write unit tests for our brand new Emailvalidator class which our developer said is a good one. Let's take a look at our validator function first:

```
//class.emailvalidator.php
class EmailValidator
{
  public function validateEmail($email)
  {
    $pattern = "/[A-z0-9]{1,64}@[A-z0-9]+\.[A-z0-9]{2,3}/";
    preg_match($pattern, $email,$matches);
    return (strlen($matches[0])==strlen($email)?true:false);
  }
}
?>
```

And here comes our test case:

```
class TestEmailValidator extends PHPUnit_Framework_TestCase
{
  private $Ev;
  protected function setup()
  {
    $this->Ev = new EmailValidator();
  }
  protected  function tearDown()
  {
    unset($this->Ev);
  }
  public function testSimpleEmail()
  {
    $result = $this->Ev->validateEmail("has.in@somewherein.net");
    $this->assertTrue($result);
  }
}
```

Now you have to write the test suit and run:

```
$suite = new PHPUnit_Framework_TestSuite();
$suite->addTestSuite("TestEmailValidator");
PHPUnit_TextUI_TestRunner::run($suite);
```

You will get the following output when you run this test suite:

```
PHPUnit 3.0.5 by Sebastian Bergmann.

...

Time: 00:00

OK (1 test)
```

Now try harder; try to break your code. Try all the possible cases that may occur in an email and try as many as you can. We are going to add more test cases:

```
class TestEmailValidator extends PHPUnit_Framework_TestCase
{
  private $Ev;
  protected function setUp()
  {
    $this->Ev = new EmailValidator();
  }
  protected  function tearDown()
  {
```

```php
      unset($this->Ev);
  }
  public function testSimpleEmail()
  {
    $result = $this->Ev->validateEmail("hasin@somewherein.net");
    $this->assertTrue($result);
  }
  public function testEmailWithDotInName()
  {
    $result = $this->Ev->validateEmail("has.in@somewherein.net");
    $this->assertTrue($result);
  }
  public function testEmailWithComma()
  {
    $result = $this->Ev->validateEmail("has,in@somewherein.net");
    $this->assertFalse($result);
  }
  public function testEmailWithSpace()
  {
    $result = $this->Ev->validateEmail("has in@somewherein.net");
    $this->assertTrue($result);
  }
  public function testEmailLengthMoreThan64Char()
  {
    $result =
    $this->Ev->validateEmail(str_repeat("h",67)."@somewherein.net");
    $this->assertFalse($result);
  }
  public function testEmailWithInValidCharacters()
  {
    $result = $this->Ev->validateEmail("has#in@somewherein.net");
    $this->assertFalse($result);
  }
  public function testEmailWithNoDomain()
  {
    $result = $this->Ev->validateEmail("hasin@");
    $this->assertFalse($result);
  }
  public function testEmailWithInvalidDomain()
  {
    $result =
       $this->Ev->validateEmail("hasin@somewherein.comnetorg");
    $this->assertFalse($result);
  }
}
```

When you run the test suite, you will get the following result:

```
PHPUnit 3.0.5 by Sebastian Bergmann.
.F.F....
Time: 00:00
There were 1 failures:
1) testEmailWithDotInName(TestEmailValidator)
Failed asserting that <boolean:false> is identical to <boolean:true>.
C:\OOP with PHP5\Codes\ch5\UnitTest\EmailValidatorTest.php:40
C:\OOP with PHP5\Codes\ch5\UnitTest\EmailValidatorTest.php:83
C:\Program Files\Zend\ZendStudio-5.2.0\bin\php5\dummy.php:1
FAILURES!
Tests: 8, Failures: 1.
```

So our email validator fails! If you look at the result you will see that it fails with `testEmailWithDotInName`. Therefore, we have to change the regular expression pattern we used and allow . in the name.

Let's redesign the validator as show here:

```php
class EmailValidator
{
  public function validateEmail($email)
  {
    $pattern = "/[A-z0-9\.]{1,64}@[A-z0-9]+\.[A-z0-9]{2,3}/";
    preg_match($pattern, $email,$matches);
    return (strlen($matches[0])==strlen($email)?true:false);
  }
}
```

Now if you run your test suites again, you will see the following output:

```
PHPUnit 3.0.5 by Sebastian Bergmann.

........
Time: 00:00
OK (8 tests)
```

Our test passes.

So what is the benefit? Time after time, when you need to add new validation rules to your regular expression, this unit test will help to do the regression test so that the same fault never occurs again.

That's the beauty of Unit Testing.

You will find two functions named setUp() and tearDown() in the above example. setUp() is used for setting up everything for the test; you can use it to connect to DB, to open a file or something similar. tearDown() is for cleaning. It is called when the script finishes executing.

Unit Testing for Everyday Script

Alongside these unit tests for functions and small classes, you will need to write unit tests for a final result achieved by different functions. However, as specific you go with your unit tests, the better outcome you can expect. Do also remember that of the many unit tests you write, only few of them are actually useful.

Now we will discuss how to test routines that works with a database. Let us create a small class which inserts, finds and updates the record, which we will write unit tests for. Here comes our small class, which directly interacts with a table named users in our database.

```php
<?
class DB
{
  private $connection;
  public function __construct()
  {
    $this->connection = mysql_connect("localhost","root","root1234");
    mysql_select_db("test",$this->connection);
  }
  public function insertData($data)
  {
    $fields = join(array_keys($data),",");
    $values = "'".join(array_values($data),",")."'";
    $query = "INSERT INTO users({$fields}) values({$values})";
    return mysql_query($query, $this->connection);
  }
  public function deleteData($id)
  {
    $query = "delete from users where id={$id}";
    return mysql_query($query, $this->connection);
  }
  public function updateData($id, $data)
  {
    $queryparts = array();
    foreach ($data as $key=>$value)
```

```
    {
      $queryparts[] = "{$key} = '{$value}'";
    }
    $query = "UPDATE users SET ".join($queryparts,",")."
                                        WHERE id='{$id}'";
    return mysql_query($query, $this->connection);
  }
}
?>
```

We need to test all the public methods in this class to ensure they are working properly. So here come our test cases.

```
<?
require_once "PHPUnit/Framework/TestCase.php";

class DBTester extends PHPUnit_Framework_TestCase
{
  private $connection;
  private $Db;
  protected function setup()
  {
    $this->Db = new DB();
    $this->connection = mysql_connect("localhost","root","root1234");
    mysql_select_db("abcd",$this->connection);
  }
  protected  function tearDown()
  {
    mysql_close($this->connection);
  }
  public function testValidInsert()
  {
    $data = array("name"=>"afif","pass"=>md5("hello world"));
    mysql_query("delete from users");
    $result = $this->Db->insertData($data);
    $this->assertNotNull($result);
    $affected_rows = mysql_affected_rows($this->connection);
    $this->assertEquals(1, $affected_rows);
  }
  public function testInvalidInsert()
  {
    $data = array("names"=>"afif","passwords"=>md5("hello world"));
    mysql_query("delete from users");
    $result = $this->Db->insertData($data);
```

```
      $this->assertNotNull($result);
      $affected_rows = mysql_affected_rows($this->connection);
      $this->assertEquals(-1, $affected_rows);
   }
   public function testUpdate()
   {
      $data = array("name"=>"afif","pass"=>md5("hello world"));
      mysql_query("truncate table users");
      $this->Db->insertData($data);
      $data = array("name"=>"afif2","pass"=>md5("hello world"));
      $result = $this->Db->updateData(1, $data);
      $this->assertNotNull($result);
      $affected_rows = mysql_affected_rows($this->connection);
      $this->assertEquals(1, $affected_rows);
   }
   public function testDelete()
   {
      $data = array("name"=>"afif","pass"=>md5("hello world"));
mysql_query("truncate table users");
      $this->Db->insertData($data);
      $result = $this->Db->deleteData(1);
      $this->assertNotNull($result);
      $affected_rows = mysql_affected_rows($this->connection);
      $this->assertEquals(1, $affected_rows);
   }
}
?>
```

The test suite is like this:

```
<?
require_once 'PHPUnit/TextUI/TestRunner.php';
require_once "PHPUnit/Framework/TestSuite.php";
$suite = new PHPUnit_Framework_TestSuite();
$suite->addTestSuite("DBTester");
PHPUnit_TextUI_TestRunner::run($suite);

?>
```

So what result will you get?

```
PHPUnit 3.0.5 by Sebastian Bergmann.

. . . .

Time: 00:00

OK (4 tests)
```

However, these are basic functionality tests. We must make more versatile tests and find out how our objects may fail. Let's add two more tests as shown below:

```php
public function testInvalidUpdate()
    {
        $data = array("name"=>"afif","pass"=>md5("hello world"));
        mysql_query("truncate table users");
        $this->Db->insertData($data);
        $data = array("name"=>"afif2","pass"=>md5("hello world"));
        $result = $this->Db->updateData(2, $data);
        $affected_rows = mysql_affected_rows($this->connection);
        $this->assertEquals(0, $affected_rows);
}
    public function testInvalidDelete()
    {
        $data = array("name"=>"afif","pass"=>md5("hello world"));
        mysql_query("truncate table users");
        $this->Db->insertData($data);
        $result = $this->Db->deleteData("*");
        $this->assertNotNull($result);
        $affected_rows = mysql_affected_rows($this->connection);
        $this->assertEquals(-1, $affected_rows);
    }
```

Now if you run the test suite you will get the following result:

```
PHPUnit 3.0.5 by Sebastian Bergmann.

. . . . . .

Time: 00:00

OK (6 tests)
```

Our DB code is looking hard to break.

In real life unit testing, you need to think beyond how you can break your own code. If you can write unit tests that break your existing code, that's better.

Test Driven Development

Now it's time to go further into unit testing. You may ask when you need to write unit tests before coding for applications: during time of development, or after finishing coding? Well, developers from different corners have different things to say, however it is found to be more useful to write the test first and then go for a real application. This is called **Test Driven Development** or **TDD** in short. TDD helps you to design better API for your application.

You may ask how to write tests when you don't have any real code, and which things to test? You don't need real objects for TDD. Just imagine some mock objects, which have just the functions. You will use those functions with the imaginary result. You can also write incomplete tests, which means a test with blank body. At your own convenience, you can write you can write the content of the test. Let's see the following example to understand how unit testing before real code actually fits in project development.

PHPUnit provides you a lot of useful API for test-first programming such as `markTestSkipped()` and `markTestIncomplete()`. We will use these two methods to mark some of our tests, which are not implemented. Let us design a small feedback manager which can accept user's feedback and mail them to you. So what could be the useful features of a feedback manager? I would suggest the following:

- It can render a feedback form.
- It will handle user's input and properly filter it.
- It will have a spam prevention functionality.
- It will prevent any automated feedback submitted by bots or spammers.
- It will render a confirmation after submission of feedback, mailing it to owner.

Let's create some blank unit tests for this. Here comes our test case, before we have the real code:

```
<?
class FeedbackTester extends PHPUnit_Framework_TestCase
{
  public function testUsersEmail()
  {
    $this->markTestIncomplete();
  }
  public function testInvalidDomain()
  {
    $this->markTestIncomplete();
  }
```

```php
  public function testCaptchaGenerator()
  {
    $this->markTestIncomplete();
  }
  public function testCaptchaChecker()
  {
    $this->markTestIncomplete();
  }
  public function testFormRenderer()
  {
    $this->markTestIncomplete();
  }
  public function testFormHandler()
  {
    $this->markTestIncomplete();
  }
  public function testValidUserName()
  {
    $this->markTestIncomplete();
  }
  public function testValidSubject()
  {
    $this->markTestIncomplete();
  }
  public function testValidContent()
  {
    $this->markTestIncomplete();
  }
  public function testFeedbackSender()
  {
    $this->markTestIncomplete();
  }
  public function testConfirmer()
  {
    $this->markTestIncomplete();
  }
}
?>
```

This is good; we have now created 11 blank tests. Now if you run this test case using test suite, you will get the following result:

```
PHPUnit 3.0.5 by Sebastian Bergmann.

IIIIIIIIIII

Time: 00:00

OK, but incomplete or skipped tests!
Tests: 11, Incomplete: 11.
```

PHPUnit successfully figured out that all our tests are marked as incomplete. Now let's think again. If you generate an `InputValidator` object, which validates user input and filters all malicious data from it, then we may have only one test case, `testValidInput()` instead of all these `testValidUserName()`, `testValidSubject()`, `testValidContent()`. So we can skip those tests. Now let's create the new test routine `testValidInput()` and mark it as incomplete:

```
public function testValidInput()
{
  $this->markTestIncomplete();
}
```

What will we do with those three tests that we plan to skip? We will not delete them but mark them as skipped. Modify the line `$this->markTestIncomplete()` to `$this->markTestSkipped()`. For example:

```
public function testValidUserName()
{
  $this->markTestSkipped();
}
```

Now if you run your test suite again you will get the following result:

```
PHPUnit 3.0.5 by Sebastian Bergmann.
IIIIIISSSIII
Time: 00:00

OK, but incomplete or skipped tests!
Tests: 12, Incomplete: 9, Skipped: 3.
```

PHPUnit is showing that it skipped three tests.

To keep our discussion short and focussed, we will now implement only one test from these nine. We will test that the feedback form renderer is actually working fine.

Now here is our revised test routine `testFormRenderer()` in our test case.

```
public function testFormRenderer(){
  $testResult = true;
  $message = "";
  $Fm= new FeedbackManager();
  ob_start();
  $Fm->renderFeedbackForm();
  $output = ob_get_clean();
  if (strpos($output, "name='email'")===false && $testResult==true)
  list($testResult, $message) = array(false,
                            "Email field is not present");
```

```
    if (strpos($output, "name='username'")===false &&
                                    $testResult==true)
    list($testResult, $message) = array(false,
                        "Username is field not present");
    if (strpos($output, "name='subject'")===false && $testResult==true)
    list($testResult, $message) = array(false,
                              "Subject field is not present");
    if (strpos($output, "name='message'")===false && $testResult==true)
    list($testResult, $message) = array(false,
                              "Message field is not present");
    $this->assertTrue($testResult, $message);
    //$this->markTestIncomplete();
}
```

It clearly states that in our feedback manager there must be a method named
`renderFeedbackForm()` and in the generated output there must be four input
fields namely, `email`,`subject`,`username` and `message`. Now let's create our
`FeedBackManager` object. Here is `FeedBackManager` with a single method to render
a feedback form:

```
class FeedBackManager
<?
{
  public function renderFeedbackForm()
  {
    $form = <<< END
    <form method=POST action="">
      Name: <br/>
      <input type='text' name='username'><br/>
      Email: <br/>
      <input type='text' name='email'><br/>
      Subject: <br/>
      <input type='text' name='subject'><br/>
      <input type='submit' value='submit>
    </form>
    END;
    echo $form;
  }
}
?>
```

Now if you run the unit test suite you will get the following result:

```
PHPUnit 3.0.5 by Sebastian Bergmann.
IIIIFISSSIII
Time: 00:00
There was 1 failure:
1) testFormRenderer(FeedbackTester)
Message field is not present
Failed asserting that <boolean:false> is identical to <boolean:true>.
C:\OOP with PHP5\Codes\ch5\UnitTest\BlankTest.php:52
C:\OOP with PHP5\Codes\ch5\UnitTest\BlankTest.php:104
C:\Program Files\Zend\ZendStudio-5.2.0\bin\php5\dummy.php:1
FAILURES!
Tests: 12, Failures: 1, Incomplete: 8, Skipped: 3.
```

Our form renderer failed. Why? Take a look at the output that comes from PHPUnit. It says `Message field is not present`. Oh! We forgot to place a `textarea` object named `message`. Let's revise our `renderFeedbackForm()` method and correct it.

```
class FeedBackManager
{

  public function renderFeedbackForm()
  {
    $form = <<< END
    <form method=POST action="">
      Name: <br/>
      <input type='text' name='username'><br/>
      Email: <br/>
      <input type='text' name='email'><br/>
       Subject: <br/>
      <input type='text' name='subject'><br/>
      Message: <br/>
      <textarea name='message'></textarea><br/>
      <input type='submit' value='submit>
    </form>
END;
    echo $form;
  }
}
```

We have added the message field. Now let's run the suite again. You will get the following output:

```
PHPUnit 3.0.5 by Sebastian Bergmann.
IIII.ISSSIII
Time: 00:00

OK, but incomplete or skipped tests!
Tests: 12, Incomplete: 8, Skipped: 3.
```

Great! Our test has passed. That means our rendered form is potentially error free.

This is the style of Test Driven Development. You have to foresee your application code before it is actually written. Using TDD helps you to design good API and good code.

Writing Multiple Assertions

Don't write multiple assertions under one test. Split it as shown in the example above. To clarify, the following example is a bad example of a unit test.

```php
public function testFormRenderer(){
    $testResult = true;
    $message = "";
    $Fm = new FeedBackManager();
    ob_start();
    $Fm->renderFeedbackForm();
    $output = ob_get_clean();
    $testResult = strpos($output, "name='email'");
    $this->assertEquals(true, $testResult,
                            "Email field is not present");
    $testResult = strpos($output, "name='username'");
    $this->assertEquals(true, $testResult,
                            "Username field is not present");
    $testResult = strpos($output, "name='subject'");
    $this->assertEquals(true, $testResult,
                            "Subject field is not present");
    $testResult = strpos($output, "name='message'");
    $this->assertEquals(true, $testResult,
                            "Message field is not present");
}
```

This code will run, but multiple assertions in a single routine are prohibited and are against good application design.

PHPUnit API

There are several types of asserting API provided by PHPUnit. In our examples we used ones like `assertTrue()`, `assertEquals()`, `assertFalse()`, and `assertNotNull()`. However, there are dozens more. The function names are self explanatory. The following table is taken from the book *PHPUnit Pocket Guide* written by Sebastian Bergmann himself and published by O'Reilly. The book is made free by O'Reilly and Sebastian Bergmann under the Creative Commons License. The latest version of this book is currently available at `http://www.phpunit.de/ pocket_guide/3.0/en/index.html`.

The following table shows all the assert functions possible with PHPUnit:

Assertion	Meaning
`void assertTrue(bool $condition)`	Reports an error if `$condition` is FALSE.
`void assertTrue(bool $condition, string $message)`	Reports an error identified by `$message` if `$condition` is FALSE.
`void assertFalse(bool $condition)`	Reports an error if `$condition` is TRUE.
`void assertFalse(bool $condition, string $message)`	Reports an error identified by `$message` if `$condition` is TRUE.
`void assertNull(mixed $variable)`	Reports an error if `$variable` is not NULL.
`void assertNull(mixed $variable, string $message)`	Reports an error identified by `$message` if `$variable` is not NULL.
`void assertNotNull(mixed $variable)`	Reports an error if `$variable` is NULL.
`void assertNotNull(mixed $variable, string $message)`	Reports an error identified by `$message` if `$variable` is NULL.
`void assertSame(object $expected, object $actual)`	Reports an error if the two variables `$expected` and `$actual` do not reference the same object.
`void assertSame(object $expected, object $actual, string $message)`	Reports an error identified by `$message` if the two variables `$expected` and `$actual` do not reference the same object.
`void assertSame(mixed $expected, mixed $actual)`	Reports an error if the two variables `$expected` and `$actual` do not have the same type and value.

Assertion	Meaning
void assertSame(mixed $expected, mixed $actual, string $message)	Reports an error identified by $message if the two variables $expected and $actual do not have the same type and value.
void assertNotSame(object $expected, object $actual)	Reports an error if the two variables $expected and $actual reference the same object.
void assertNotSame(object $expected, object $actual, string $message)	Reports an error identified by $message if the two variables $expected and $actual reference the same object.
void assertNotSame(mixed $expected, mixed $actual)	Reports an error if the two variables $expected and $actual have the same type and value.
void assertNotSame(mixed $expected, mixed $actual, string $message)	Reports an error identified by $message if the two variables $expected and $actual have the same type and value.
void assertAttributeSame(object $expected, string $actualAttributeName, object $actualObject)	Reports an error if $actualObject->actualAttributeName and $actual do not reference the same object. The visibility of the $actualObject->actualAttributeName attribute may be public, protected, or private.
void assertAttributeSame(object $expected, string $actualAttributeName, object $actualObject, string $message)	Reports an error identified by $message if $actualObject->actualAttributeName and $actual do not reference the same object. The visibility of the $actualObject->actualAttributeName attribute may be public, protected, or private.
void assertAttributeSame(mixed $expected, string $actualAttributeName, object $actualObject)	Reports an error if $actualObject->actualAttributeName and $actual do not have the same type and value. The visibility of the $actualObject->actualAttributeName attribute may be public, protected, or private.

Assertion	Meaning
`void assertAttributeSame(mixed $expected, string $actualAttributeName, object $actualObject, string $message)`	Reports an error identified by `$message` if `$actualObject->actualAttributeName` and `$actual` do not have the same type and value. The visibility of the `$actualObject->actualAttributeName` attribute may be public, protected, or private.
`void assertAttributeNotSame(object $expected, string $actualAttributeName, object $actualObject)`	Reports an error if `$actualObject->actualAttributeName` and `$actual` reference the same object. The visibility of the `$actualObject->actualAttributeName` attribute may be public, protected, or private.
`void assertAttributeNotSame(object $expected, string $actualAttributeName, object $actualObject, string $message)`	Reports an error identified by `$message` if `$actualObject->actualAttributeName` and `$actual` reference the same object. The visibility of the `$actualObject->actualAttributeName` attribute may be public, protected, or private.
`void assertAttributeNotSame(mixed $expected, string $actualAttributeName, object $actualObject)`	Reports an error if `$actualObject->actualAttributeName` and `$actual` have the same type and value. The visibility of the `$actualObject->actualAttributeName` attribute may be public, protected, or private.
`void assertAttributeNotSame(mixed $expected, string $actualAttributeName, object $actualObject, string $message)`	Reports an error identified by `$message` if `$actualObject->actualAttributeName` and `$actual` have the same type and value. The visibility of the `$actualObject->actualAttributeName` attribute may be public, protected, or private.
`void assertEquals(array $expected, array $actual)`	Reports an error if the two arrays `$expected` and `$actual` are not equal.

Assertion	Meaning
void assertEquals(array $expected, array $actual, string $message)	Reports an error identified by $message if the two arrays $expected and $actual are not equal.
void assertNotEquals(array $expected, array $actual)	Reports an error if the two arrays $expected and $actual are equal.
void assertNotEquals(array $expected, array $actual, string $message)	Reports an error identified by $message if the two arrays $expected and $actual are equal.
void assertEquals(float $expected, float $actual, '', float $delta = 0)	Reports an error if the two floats $expected and $actual are not within $delta of each other.
void assertEquals(float $expected, float $actual, string $message, float $delta = 0)	Reports an error identified by $message if the two floats $expected and $actual are not within $delta of each other.
void assertNotEquals(float $expected, float $actual, '', float $delta = 0)	Reports an error if the two floats $expected and $actual are within $delta of each other.
void assertNotEquals(float $expected, float $actual, string $message, float $delta = 0)	Reports an error identified by $message if the two floats $expected and $actual are within $delta of each other.
void assertEquals(string $expected, string $actual)	Reports an error if the two strings $expected and $actual are not equal. The error is reported as the delta between the two strings.
void assertEquals(string $expected, string $actual, string $message)	Reports an error identified by $message if the two strings $expected and $actual are not equal. The error is reported as the delta between the two strings.
void assertNotEquals(string $expected, string $actual)	Reports an error if the two strings $expected and $actual are equal.
void assertNotEquals(string $expected, string $actual, string $message)	Reports an error identified by $message if the two strings $expected and $actual are equal.

Assertion	Meaning
`void assertEquals(mixed $expected, mixed $actual)`	Reports an error if the two variables `$expected` and `$actual` are not equal.
`void assertEquals(mixed $expected, mixed $actual, string $message)`	Reports an error identified by `$message` if the two variables `$expected` and `$actual` are not equal.
`void assertNotEquals(mixed $expected, mixed $actual)`	Reports an error if the two variables `$expected` and `$actual` are equal.
`void assertNotEquals(mixed $expected, mixed $actual, string $message)`	Reports an error identified by `$message` if the two variables `$expected` and `$actual` are equal.
`void assertAttributeEquals(array $expected, string $actualAttributeName, object $actualObject)`	Reports an error if the two arrays `$expected` and `$actualObject->actualAttributeName` are not equal. The visibility of the `$actualObject->actualAttributeName` attribute may be public, protected, or private.
`void assertAttributeEquals(array $expected, string $actualAttributeName, object $actualObject, string $message)`	Reports an error identified by `$message` if the two arrays `$expected` and `$actualObject->actualAttributeName` are not equal. The visibility of the `$actualObject->actualAttributeName` attribute may be public, protected, or private.
`void assertAttributeNotEquals(array $expected, string $actualAttributeName, object $actualObject)`	Reports an error if the two arrays `$expected` and `$actualObject->actualAttributeName` are equal. The visibility of the `$actualObject->actualAttributeName` attribute may be public, protected, or private.
`void assertAttributeNotEquals(array $expected, string $actualAttributeName, object $actualObject, string $message)`	Reports an error identified by `$message` if the two arrays `$expected` and `$actualObject->actualAttributeName` are equal. The visibility of the `$actualObject->actualAttributeName` attribute may be public, protected, or private.

Assertion	Meaning
`void assertAttributeEquals(float $expected, string $actualAttributeName, object $actualObject, '', float $delta = 0)`	Reports an error if the two floats `$expected` and `$actualObject->actualAttributeName` are not within `$delta` of each other. The visibility of the `$actualObject->actualAttributeName` attribute may be public, protected, or private.
`void assertAttributeEquals(float $expected, string $actualAttributeName, object $actualObject, string $message, float $delta = 0)`	Reports an error identified by `$message` if the two floats `$expected` and `$actualObject->actualAttributeName` are not within `$delta` of each other. The visibility of the `$actualObject->actualAttributeName` attribute may be public, protected, or private.
`void assertAttributeNotEquals(float $expected, string $actualAttributeName, object $actualObject, '', float $delta = 0)`	Reports an error if the two floats `$expected` and `$actualObject->actualAttributeName` are within `$delta` of each other. The visibility of the `$actualObject->actualAttributeName` attribute may be public, protected, or private.
`void assertAttributeNotEquals(float $expected, string $actualAttributeName, object $actualObject, string $message, float $delta = 0)`	Reports an error identified by `$message` if the two floats `$expected` and `$actualObject->actualAttributeName` are within `$delta` of each other. The visibility of the `$actualObject->actualAttributeName` attribute may be public, protected, or private.
`void assertAttributeEquals(string $expected, string $actualAttributeName, object $actualObject)`	Reports an error if the two strings `$expected` and `$actualObject->actualAttributeName` are not equal. The error is reported as the delta between the two strings. The visibility of the `$actualObject->actualAttributeName` attribute may be public, protected, or private.

Assertion	Meaning
void assertAttributeEquals(string $expected, string $actualAttributeName, object $actualObject, string $message)	Reports an error identified by $message if the two strings $expected and $actualObject->actualAttributeName are not equal. The error is reported as the delta between the two strings. The visibility of the $actualObject->actualAttributeName attribute may be public, protected, or private.
void assertAttributeNotEquals(string $expected, string $actualAttributeName, object $actualObject)	Reports an error if the two strings $expected and $actualObject->actualAttributeName are equal. The visibility of the $actualObject->actualAttributeName attribute may be public, protected, or private.
void assertAttributeNotEquals(string $expected, string $actualAttributeName, object $actualObject, string $message)	Reports an error identified by $message if the two strings $expected and $actualObject->actualAttributeName are equal. The visibility of the $actualObject->actualAttributeName attribute may be public, protected, or private.
void assertAttributeEquals(mixed $expected, string $actualAttributeName, object $actualObject)	Reports an error if the two variables $expected and $actualObject->actualAttributeName are not equal. The visibility of the $actualObject->actualAttributeName attribute may be public, protected, or private.
void assertAttributeEquals(mixed $expected, string $actualAttributeName, object $actualObject, string $message)	Reports an error identified by $message if the two variables $expected and $actualObject->actualAttributeName are not equal. The visibility of the $actualObject->actualAttributeName attribute may be public, protected, or private.

Assertion	Meaning
`void assertAttributeNotEquals(mixed $expected, string $actualAttributeName, object $actualObject)`	Reports an error if the two variables `$expected` and `$actualObject->actualAttributeName` are equal. The visibility of the `$actualObject->actualAttributeName` attribute may be public, protected, or private.
`void assertAttributeNotEquals(mixed $expected, string $actualAttributeName, object $actualObject, string $message)`	Reports an error identified by `$message` if the two variables `$expected` and `$actualObject->actualAttributeName` are equal. The visibility of the `$actualObject->actualAttributeName` attribute may be public, protected, or private.
`void assertContains(mixed $needle, array $expected)`	Reports an error if `$needle` is not an element of `$expected`.
`void assertContains(mixed $needle, array $expected, string $message)`	Reports an error identified by `$message` if `$needle` is not an element of `$expected`.
`void assertNotContains(mixed $needle, array $expected)`	Reports an error if `$needle` is an element of `$expected`.
`void assertNotContains(mixed $needle, array $expected, string $message)`	Reports an error identified by `$message` if `$needle` is an element of `$expected`.
`void assertContains(mixed $needle, Iterator $expected)`	Reports an error if `$needle` is not an element of `$expected`.
`void assertContains(mixed $needle, Iterator $expected, string $message)`	Reports an error identified by `$message` if `$needle` is not an element of `$expected`.
`void assertNotContains(mixed $needle, Iterator $expected)`	Reports an error if `$needle` is an element of `$expected`.
`void assertNotContains(mixed $needle, Iterator $expected, string $message)`	Reports an error identified by `$message` if `$needle` is an element of `$expected`.
`void assertContains(string $needle, string $expected)`	Reports an error if `$needle` is not a substring of `$expected`.
`void assertContains(string $needle, string $expected, string $message)`	Reports an error identified by `$message` if `$needle` is not a substring of `$expected`.

Assertion	Meaning
`void assertNotContains(string $needle, string $expected)`	Reports an error if `$needle` is a substring of `$expected`.
`void assertNotContains(string $needle, string $expected, string $message)`	Reports an error identified by `$message` if `$needle` is a substring of `$expected`.
`void assertAttributeContains(mixed $needle, string $actualAttributeName, object $actualObject)`	Reports an error if `$needle` is not an element of `$actualObject->actualAttributeName` which can be an array, a string, or an object that implements the Iterator interface. The visibility of the `$actualObject->actualAttributeName` attribute may be public, protected, or private.
`void assertAttributeContains(mixed $needle, string $actualAttributeName, object $actualObject, string $message)`	Reports an error identified by `$message` if `$needle` is not an element of `$actualObject->actualAttributeName` which can be an array, a string, or an object that implements the Iterator interface. The visibility of the `$actualObject->actualAttributeName` attribute may be public, protected, or private.
`void assertAttributeNotContains(mixed $needle, string $actualAttributeName, object $actualObject)`	Reports an error if `$needle` is an element of `$actualObject->actualAttributeName` which can be an array, a string, or an object that implements the Iterator interface. The visibility of the `$actualObject->actualAttributeName` attribute may be public, protected, or private.
`void assertAttributeNotContains(mixed $needle, string $actualAttributeName, object $actualObject, string $message)`	Reports an error identified by `$message` if `$needle` is an element of `$actualObject->actualAttributeName` which can be an array, a string, or an object that implements the Iterator interface. The visibility of the `$actualObject->actualAttributeName` attribute may be public, protected, or private.

Assertion	Meaning
`void assertRegExp(string $pattern, string $string)`	Reports an error if `$string` does not match the regular expression `$pattern`.
`void assertRegExp(string $pattern, string $string, string $message)`	Reports an error identified by `$message` if `$string` does not match the regular expression `$pattern`.
`void assertNotRegExp(string $pattern, string $string)`	Reports an error if `$string` matches the regular expression `$pattern`.
`void assertNotRegExp(string $pattern, string $string, string $message)`	Reports an error identified by `$message` if `$string` matches the regular expression `$pattern`.
`void assertType(string $expected, mixed $actual)`	Reports an error if the variable `$actual` is not of type `$expected`..
`void assertType(string $expected, mixed $actual, string $message)`	Reports an error identified by `$message` if the variable `$actual` is not of type `$expected`.
`void assertNotType(string $expected, mixed $actual)`	Reports an error if the variable `$actual` is of type `$expected`.
`void assertNotType(string $expected, mixed $actual, string $message)`	Reports an error identified by `$message` if the variable `$actual` is of type `$expected`.
`void assertFileExists(string $filename)`	Reports an error if the file specified by `$filename` does not exist.
`void assertFileExists(string $filename, string $message)`	Reports an error identified by `$message` if the file specified by `$filename` does not exist.
`void assertFileNotExists(string $filename)`	Reports an error if the file specified by `$filename` exists.
`void assertFileNotExists(string $filename, string $message)`	Reports an error identified by `$message` if the file specified by `$filename` exists.
`void assertObjectHasAttribute(string $attributeName, object $object)`	Reports an error if `$object->attributeName` does not exist.
`void assertObjectHasAttribute(string $attributeName, object $object, string $message)`	Reports an error identified by `$message` if `$object->attributeName` does not exist.

Assertion	Meaning
void assertObjectNotHasAttribute(string $attributeName, object $object)	Reports an error if $object->attributeName exists.
void assertObjectNotHasAttribute(string $attributeName, object $object, string $message)	Reports an error if $object->attributeName exists.

Summary

This chapter focuses on two very important features of object oriented programming in PHP. One is reflection, which is a part of all major programming languages like Java, Ruby, and Python. The second one is unit testing, which is an essential part of good, stable, and manageable application design. We focused on one very popular package, which is a port of JUnit in PHP, named PHPUnit. If you follow the guideline provided in this chapter you will be able to design your unit tests successfully.

In the next chapter, we will learn about some built-in objects in PHP which will make your life much easier than usual. We will learn about the huge object repository called Standard PHP Library or SPL. Before that, enjoy the debugging by writing your own unit tests.

6
Standard PHP Library

PHP5 made a developer's life a lot easier than before by introducing a number of built-in objects. These objects simplify tasks and saves countless sleepless nights for a lot of coders like me. **Standard PHP Library** (**SPL**) is a set of objects for PHP developers introduced in PHP5. They come with a lot of interfaces and objects to simplify your coding. In this chapter we will go through some of them and show you their use.

Available Objects in SPL

You can find out the available objects in SPL by executing the following code.

```php
<?php
// a simple foreach() to traverse the SPL class names
foreach(spl_classes() as $key=>$value)
  {
    echo $value."\n";
  }
?>
```

The result will show you all the available classes in your current PHP install:

```
AppendIterator
ArrayIterator
ArrayObject
BadFunctionCallException
BadMethodCallException
CachingIterator
Countable
DirectoryIterator
DomainException
EmptyIterator
FilterIterator
```

```
InfiniteIterator
InvalidArgumentException
IteratorIterator
LengthException
LimitIterator
LogicException
NoRewindIterator
OuterIterator
OutOfBoundsException
OutOfRangeException
OverflowException
ParentIterator
RangeException
RecursiveArrayIterator
RecursiveCachingIterator
RecursiveDirectoryIterator
RecursiveFilterIterator
RecursiveIterator
RecursiveIteratorIterator
RuntimeException
SeekableIterator
SimpleXMLIterator
SplFileObject
SplObjectStorage
SplObserver
SplSubject
UnderflowException
UnexpectedValueException
```

ArrayObject

This is a fantastic object introduced in SPL to simplify array operation and to enrich the normal PHP array. You can use `ArrayObject` as a simple array however internally you can enhance it and add new functionalities gradually. In this section we will see the properties and methods supported by this object. Also, we will design an enhanced `ArrayObject` for easier array access.

Here are the public members of this class:

- `__construct ($array, $flags=0, $iterator_class="ArrayIterator")`
- `append ($value)`
- `asort ()`
- `count ()`

- exchangeArray ($array)
- getArrayCopy ()
- getFlags ()
- getIterator ()
- getIteratorClass ()
- ksort ()
- natcasesort ()
- natsort ()
- offsetExists ($index)
- offsetGet ($index)
- offsetSet ($index, $newval)
- offsetUnset ($index)
- setFlags ($flags)
- setIteratorClass ($itertor_class)
- uasort (mixed cmp_function)
- uksort (mixed cmp_function)

Many of these functions are also available for array operation. Here is a brief introduction about some functions, which are differentl to those from array functions:

Function	Feature
exchangeArray ($array)	This function replaces the internal array of an ArrayObject with the new one and returns the old one.
getArrayCopy()	This function returns a copy of the internal array from inside this ArrayObject.
getIteratorClass()	This function returns the name of the Iterator class. If you don't explicitly set any other Iterator class for this object, you will always get ArrayIterator as the result.
setIteratorClass()	Using this function you can set any Iterator class as the Iterator for array object. However there is one limitation; is one limitation; this Iterator class must extend the arrayIterator class.
setFlags()	This function sets some bitwise flags to ArrayObject. Flags are 0 or 1. 0, which means properties of the object have their normal functionality when accessed as list (var_dump, foreach, etc.) and 1 means array indices can be accessed as properties in read/write.

In the interesting example shown below, we are extending `ArrayObject` and creating a more flexible `ExtendedArrayObject` for prototype like functionality. The extended array provides easier traversing through the collection. Let's have a look:

```php
<?
class ExtendedArrayObject extends ArrayObject {
  private $_array;
  public function __construct()
  {
    if (is_array(func_get_arg(0)))
    $this->_array = func_get_arg(0);
    else
    $this->_array = func_get_args();
    parent::__construct($this->_array);
  }
  public function each($callback)
  {
    $iterator = $this->getIterator();
    while($iterator->valid())
    {
      $callback($iterator->current());
      $iterator->next();
    }
  }
  public function without()
  {
    $args = func_get_args();
    return array_values(array_diff($this->_array,$args));
  }
  public function first()
  {
    return $this->_array[0];
  }
  public function indexOf($value)
  {
    return array_search($value,$this->_array);
  }
  public function inspect()
  {
    echo "<pre>".print_r($this->_array, true)."</pre>";
  }
  public function last()
  {
```

```php
    return $this->_array[count($this->_array)-1];
  }
  public function reverse($applyToSelf=false)
  {
    if (!$applyToSelf)
    return array_reverse($this->_array);
    else
    {
      $_array = array_reverse($this->_array);
      $this->_array = $_array;
      parent::__construct($this->_array);
      return $this->_array;
    }
  }
  public function shift()
  {
    $_element = array_shift($this->_array);
    parent::__construct($this->_array);
    return $_element;
  }
  public function pop()
  {
    $_element = array_pop($this->_array);
    parent::__construct($this->_array);
    return $_element;
  }
}
?>
```

If you want to see how to use it, here it goes:

```php
<?
include_once("ExtendedArrayObject.class.php");
function speak($value)
{
  echo $value;
}
$newArray = new ExtendedArrayObject(array(1,2,3,4,5,6));
/* or you can use this */
$newArray = new ExtendedArrayObject(1,2,3,4,5,6);
$newArray->each(speak); //pass callback for loop
print_r($newArray->without(2,3,4)); //subtract
$newArray->inspect(); //display the array in a nice manner
```

```
echo $newArray->indexOf(5); //position by value
print_r($newArray->reverse()); //reverse the array
print_r($newArray->reverse(true)); /*for changing array itself*/
echo $newArray->shift();//shifts the first value of the array
                         //and returns it
echo $newArray->pop();// pops out the last value of array
echo $newArray->last();
echo $newArray->first(); //the first element
?>
```

The result looks like this:

```
123456
Array
(
    [0] => 1
    [1] => 5
    [2] => 6
)
Array
(
    [0] => 1
    [1] => 2
    [2] => 3
    [3] => 4
    [4] => 5
    [5] => 6
)
4
Array
(
    [0] => 6
    [1] => 5
    [2] => 4
    [3] => 3
    [4] => 2
    [5] => 1
)
Array
(
    [0] => 6
    [1] => 5
    [2] => 4
    [3] => 3
    [4] => 2
    [5] => 1
)
6125
```

ArrayIterator

`ArrayIterator` is used to iterate over the elements of an array. In SPL, `ArrayObject` has a built-in Iterator, which you can access using `getIterator` function. You can use this object to iterate over any collection. Let's take a look at the example here:

```php
<?php
$fruits = array(
    "apple" => "yummy",
    "orange" => "ah ya, nice",
    "grape" => "wow, I love it!",
    "plum" => "nah, not me"
);

$obj = new ArrayObject( $fruits );

$it = $obj->getIterator();

// How many items are we iterating over?
echo "Iterating over: " . $obj->count() . " values\n";

// Iterate over the values in the ArrayObject:
while( $it->valid() )
{
    echo $it->key() . "=" . $it->current() . "\n";
    $it->next();
}
?>
```

This will output the following:

```
Iterating over: 4 values
apple=yummy
orange=ah ya, nice
grape=wow, I love it!
plum=nah, not me
```

However, an Iterator also implements the `IteratorAggregator` interface so you can even use them in the `foreach()` loop.

```php
<?php
$fruits = array(
    "apple" => "yummy",
    "orange" => "ah ya, nice",
    "grape" => "wow, I love it!",
    "plum" => "nah, not me"
);

$obj = new ArrayObject( $fruits );
```

```php
$it = $obj->getIterator();
// How many items are we iterating over?
echo "Iterating over: " . $obj->count() . " values\n";
// Iterate over the values in the ArrayObject:
foreach ($it as $key=>$val)
echo $key.":".$val."\n";
?>
```

You will get the same output as the previous one.

If you want to implement Iterator to your own collection, collection, I recommend you take a look at Chapter 3. If you want to know how to implement IteratorAggregator, here is an example for you:

```php
<?php
class MyArray implements IteratorAggregate
{
  private $arr;
  public function __construct()
  {
    $this->arr = array();
  }
  public function add( $key, $value )
  {
    if( $this->check( $key, $value ) )
      {
        $this->arr[$key] = $value;
      }
  }
  private function check( $key, $value )
    {
      if( $key == $value )
        {
          return false;
        }
        return true;
    }

  public function getIterator()
  {
    return new ArrayIterator( $this->arr );
  }
}
?>
```

Please note that if key and value are the same, it will not return that value while iterating. You can use it like this:

```php
<?php
$obj = new MyArray();
$obj->add( "redhat","www.redhat.com" );
$obj->add( "php", "php" );
$it = $obj->getIterator();
while( $it->valid() )
{
  echo $it->key() . "=" . $it->current() . "\n";
  $it->next();
}
?>
```

The output is:

```
redhat=www.redhat.com
```

DirectoryIterator

Another very interesting class introduced in PHP5 is `DirectoryIterator`. This object can iterate through the items present in a directory (well, those nothing but files) and you can retrieve different attributes of that file using this object.

In the PHP Manual this object is not well documented. So if you want to know the structure of this object and supported methods and properties, you can use `ReflectionClass` for that. Remember the `ReflectionClass` we used in the previous chapter? Let's take a look at the following example:

```php
<?php
ReflectionClass::export(DirectoryIterator);
?>
```

The result is:

```
Class [ <internal:SPL> <iterateable> class DirectoryIterator
                       implements Iterator, Traversable ]
{
  - Constants [0] { }
  - Static properties [0] {   }
  - Static methods [0] {   }
  - Properties [0] {   }
  - Methods [27]
{
    Method [ <internal> <ctor> public method __construct ]
{
      - Parameters [1]
{
```

```
            Parameter #0 [ <required> $path ]
        }
    }
    Method [ <internal> public method rewind ] {      }
    Method [ <internal> public method valid ] {       }
    Method [ <internal> public method key ] {      }
    Method [ <internal> public method current ] {      }
    Method [ <internal> public method next ] {      }
    Method [ <internal> public method getPath ] {      }
    Method [ <internal> public method getFilename ] {      }
    Method [ <internal> public method getPathname ] {      }
    Method [ <internal> public method getPerms ] {      }
    Method [ <internal> public method getInode ] {      }
    Method [ <internal> public method getSize ] {      }
    Method [ <internal> public method getOwner ] {      }
    Method [ <internal> public method getGroup ] {      }
    Method [ <internal> public method getATime ] {      }
    Method [ <internal> public method getMTime ] {      }
    Method [ <internal> public method getCTime ] {      }
    Method [ <internal> public method getType ] {      }
    Method [ <internal> public method isWritable ] {      }
    Method [ <internal> public method isReadable ] {      }
    Method [ <internal> public method isExecutable ] {      }
    Method [ <internal> public method isFile ] {      }
    Method [ <internal> public method isDir ] {      }
    Method [ <internal> public method isLink ] {      }
    Method [ <internal> public method isDot ] {      }
    Method [ <internal> public method openFile ]
        {
        - Parameters [3] {
          Parameter #0 [ <optional> $open_mode ]
          Parameter #1 [ <optional> $use_include_path ]
          Parameter #2 [ <optional> $context ]
          }
        }
    Method [ <internal> public method __toString ] {      }
    }
}
```

We have a handful of useful methods here. Let's make use of them. In the following example we will just create a directory crawler, which will display all files and directories in a specific drive. Take a look at one of my directories on the C drive called spket:

Now, if you run the following code, you will get the list of files and directories inside it:

```
<?
$DI = new DirectoryIterator("c:/spket");
foreach ($DI as $file) {
  echo $file."\n";
}
?>
```

The output is:

```
.

..

plugins
features
readme
.eclipseproduct
epl-v10.html
notice.html
startup.jar
configuration
spket.exe
spket.ini
```

But the output doesn't make any sense. Can you detect which are the directories and which are the files? It's very difficult, so let's make the result useful for us.

```php
<?
$DI = new DirectoryIterator("c:/spket");
$directories = array();
$files = array();
foreach ($DI as $file) {
  $filename = $file->getFilename();
  if ($file->isDir()){
    if(strpos($filename,".")===false)
    $directories[] = $filename;
  }
  else
  $files[] = $filename;
}
echo "Directories\n";
print_r($directories);
echo "\nFiles\n";
print_r($files);
?>
```

The output is:

```
Directories
Array
(
    [1] => plugins
    [2] => features
    [3] => readme
    [4] => configuration
)

Files
Array
(
    [0] => .eclipseproduct
    [1] => epl-v10.html
    [2] => notice.html
    [3] => startup.jar
    [4] => spket.exe
    [5] => spket.ini
)
```

You may ask at this point, if there is a shortcut link, how you can detect it. Simple, just use the `$file->isLink()` function to detect if that file is a shortcut.

Let's take a look at other useful methods of the `DirectoryIterator` object:

Methods	Feature
`getPathname()`	Returns the absolute path name (with file name) of this file.
`getSize()`	Returns size of file in number of bytes.
`getOwner()`	Returns the owner ID.
`getATime()`	Returns the last access time in timestamp.
`getMTime()`	Returns the modification time in timestamp.
`getCTime()`	Returns the creation time in timestamp.
`getType()`	Returns either "file", "dir", or "link".

Other methods are quite self explanatory, so we are not covering them here. One more thing to remember however, is `getInode()`, `getOwner()`, and `getGroup()` will return 0 in win32 machines.

RecursiveDirectoryIterator

So what is this object? Remember our previous example? We got a list of directories and files only. However, what if we want to get a list of all directories inside that directory without implementing the recursion? Then `RecursiveDirectoryIterator` is here to save your life.

The recursive directory Iterator can be used to great effect with `RecursiveIteratorIterator` to implement the recursion. Let's take a look at the following example, it traverses through all the directories under a directory (no matter how nested it is):

```php
<?php
// Create the new iterator:
$it = new RecursiveIteratorIterator(new RecursiveDirectoryIterator(
                                            'c:/spket' ));

foreach( $it as $key=>$file )
{
    echo $key."=>".$file."\n";
}
?>
```

The output is like this one:

```
c:/spket/epl-v10.html=>epl-v10.html
c:/spket/notice.html=>notice.html
c:/spket/startup.jar=>startup.jar
c:/spket/configuration/config.ini=>config.ini
c:/spket/configuration/org.eclipse.osgi/.manager/
                          .fileTableLock=>.fileTableLock
c:/spket/configuration/org.eclipse.osgi/.manager/
                          .fileTable.4=>.fileTable.4
c:/spket/configuration/org.eclipse.osgi/.manager/
                          .fileTable.5=>.fileTable.5
c:/spket/configuration/org.eclipse.osgi/bundles/4/1/.cp/
                 swt-win32-3236.dll=>swt-win32-3236.dll
c:/spket/configuration/org.eclipse.osgi/bundles/4/1/.cp/
                 swt-gdip-win32-3236.dll=>swt-gdip-win32-3236.dll
c:/spket/configuration/org.eclipse.osgi/bundles/48/1/.cp/os/win32/
                 x86/localfile_1_0_0.dll=>localfile_1_0_0.dll
c:/spket/configuration/org.eclipse.osgi/bundles/69/1/.cp/os/win32/
                 x86/monitor.dll=>monitor.dll
c:/spket/spket.exe=>spket.exe
c:/spket/spket.ini=>spket.ini
.........
```

I can hear you asking yourself: 'why are these useless files printed here?' Just take a look at directory structure and see how it retrieves the entire file name with their path as key.

RecursiveIteratorIterator

To recursively iterate over a collection, you can make take advantage of this object introduced in SPL. Let's take a look at the following example to understand how effectively it can be used in your everyday programming. In the previous sections and also in the coming sections we see many examples using `RecursiveIteratorIterator`; so we are not giving any more examples in this section.

AppendIterator

If you want to use a collection of Iterators to iterate through, then this could be your life saver. This object saves all the Iterators in a collection and iterates through all of them at once.

Let's take a look at the following example of `append` Iterator, where we traverse through a collection of Iterators and then minimize the code:

```php
<?
class Post
{
  public $id;
  public $title;
  function __construct($title, $id)
  {
    $this->title = $title;
    $this->id = $id;
  }
}
class Comment{
  public $content;
  public $post_id;
  function __construct($content, $post_id)
  {
    $this->content = $content;
    $this->post_id = $post_id;
  }
}
$posts = new ArrayObject();
$comments = new ArrayObject();

$posts->append(new post("Post 1",1));
$posts->append(new post("Post 2",2));
$comments->append(new Comment("comment 1",1));
$comments->append(new Comment("comment 2",1));
$comments->append(new Comment("comment 3",2));
$comments->append(new Comment("comment 4",2));
$a = new AppendIterator();
$a->append($posts->getIterator());
$a->append($comments->getIterator());
//print_r($a->getInnerIterator());
foreach ($a as $key=>$val)
{
  if ($val instanceof post)
  echo "title = {$val->title}\n";
  else if ($val instanceof Comment )
  echo "content = {$val->content}\n";
}
?>
```

And here comes the output:

```
title = Post 1
title = Post 2
content = comment 1
content = comment 2
content = comment 3
content = comment 4
```

FilterIterator

As its name suggests, this Iterator helps you to filter out the result through iteration so that you get only the results you require. This Iterator is very useful for iteration with filtering,

FilterIterator exposes two extra methods over a regular Iterator. One is accept() which is called every time in internal iteration and is your key point to perform the filter. The second one is getInnerIterator(), which returns the current Iterator inside this FilterIterator.

In this example we use FilterIterator to filter out data while traversing through a collection.

```php
<?php
class GenderFilter extends FilterIterator
{
  private $GenderFilter;
  public function __construct( Iterator $it, $gender="F" )
  {
    parent::__construct( $it );
    $this->GenderFilter = $gender;
  }
  //your key point to implement filter
  public function accept()
  {
    $person = $this->getInnerIterator()->current();
    if( $person['sex'] == $this->GenderFilter )
    {
      return TRUE;
    }
    return FALSE;
  }
}
$arr = array(
```

```
    array("name"=>"John Abraham", "sex"=>"M", "age"=>27),
    array("name"=>"Lily Bernard", "sex"=>"F", "age"=>37),
    array("name"=>"Ayesha Siddika", "sex"=>"F", "age"=>26),
    array("name"=>"Afif", "sex"=>"M", "age"=>2)
);
$persons = new ArrayObject( $arr );
$iterator = new GenderFilter( $persons->getIterator() );
foreach( $iterator as $person )
{
  echo $person['name'] . "\n";
}
echo str_repeat("-",30)."\n";
$persons = new ArrayObject( $arr );
$iterator = new GenderFilter( $persons->getIterator() ,"M");
foreach( $iterator as $person )
{
    echo $person['name'] . "\n";
}
?>
```

If you run the code, you will get the following result:

```
Lily Bernard
Ayesha Siddika
------------------------------
John Abraham
Afif
```

I'm sure you will agree that this is quite interesting, however did you get the catch? This is filtered by the following entry point:

```
public function accept()
  {
    $person = $this->getInnerIterator()->current();
    if( $person['sex'] == $this->GenderFilter )
    {
      return TRUE;
    }
      return FALSE;
  }
}
```

LimitIterator

What if you want to define the start point from where your iteration will start and also define the times you want to iterate? This is made possible using `LimitIterator`.

`LimitIterator` takes three parameters while constructing. The first one is a regular Iterator, the second one is the starting offset, and the third one is the number of times that it will iterate. Take a look at the following example:

```
<?
$arr = array(
   array("name"=>"John Abraham", "sex"=>"M", "age"=>27),
   array("name"=>"Lily Bernard", "sex"=>"F", "age"=>37),
   array("name"=>"Ayesha Siddika", "sex"=>"F", "age"=>26),
   array("name"=>"Afif", "sex"=>"M", "age"=>2)
);
$persons = new ArrayObject($arr);
$LI = new LimitIterator($persons->getIterator(),1,2);
foreach ($LI as $person) {
   echo $person['name']."\n";
}
?>
```

And the output is:

```
Lily Bernard
Ayesha Siddika
```

NoRewindIterator

This is another Iterator in which you can't invoke the `rewind` method. That means it is a forward-only Iterator, which can read a collection only once. Take a look at the structure; if you execute the following code you will get the methods supported by this Iterator:

```
<?
print_r(get_class_methods(NoRewindIterator));
   //you can also use refelection API as before to see the methods.
?>
```

The output would be the methods, as seen below:

```
Array
(
   [0] => __construct
   [1] => rewind
   [2] => valid
   [3] => key
   [4] => current
   [5] => next
   [6] => getInnerIterator
)
```

Surprisingly, it has no rewind method, but you can see it, can't you? Well, that method has no implementation, it is empty. It is there as it implements the Iterator interface, but there is no implementation of that function, so you can't rewind.

```
<?
$arr = array(
   array("name"=>"John Abraham", "sex"=>"M", "age"=>27),
   array("name"=>"Lily Bernard", "sex"=>"F", "age"=>37),
   array("name"=>"Ayesha Siddika", "sex"=>"F", "age"=>26),
   array("name"=>"Afif", "sex"=>"M", "age"=>2)
);
$persons = new ArrayObject($arr);
$LI = new NoRewindIterator($persons->getIterator());
foreach ($LI as $person) {
   echo $person['name']."\n";
   $LI->rewind();
}
?>
```

If the `rewind()` method works, this code will be an endless loop. But in practical, it displays the output as shown below:

```
John Abraham
Lily Bernard
Ayesha Siddika
Afif
```

SeekableIterator

This is an interface introduced in SPL, which many Iterator classes actually implement internally. If this interface is implemented, you can perform `seek()` operation inside this array.

Let's take a look at the following example where we implement `SeekableIterator` to provide a searching facility over a collection:

```
<?
$arr = array(
    array("name"=>"John Abraham", "sex"=>"M", "age"=>27),
    array("name"=>"Lily Bernard", "sex"=>"F", "age"=>37),
    array("name"=>"Ayesha Siddika", "sex"=>"F", "age"=>26),
    array("name"=>"Afif", "sex"=>"M", "age"=>2)
);

$persons = new ArrayObject($arr);

$it = $persons->getIterator();
$it->seek(2);
while ($it->valid())
{
  print_r($it->current());
   $it->next();
}
?>
```

The output is:

```
Array
(
   [name] => Ayesha Siddika
   [sex] => F
   [age] => 26
)
Array
(
   [name] => Afif
   [sex] => M
   [age] => 2
)
```

RecursiveIterator

This is another interface introduced by SPL for easy recursion over nested collections. By implementing this interface and using it with `RecursiveIteratorIterator`, you can easily traverse through nested collections.

If you implement `RecursiveIterator`, you have to apply two methods, one is `hasChildren()`, which must determine whether the current object is an array or not (and that means if it has children or not) and the second one is `getChildren()`, which must return an instance of the same class over the collection. That's it. To understand the bigger picture, take a look at the following example:

```php
<?
$arr = array(
   "john"=>array("name"=>"John Abraham", "sex"=>"M", "age"=>27),
   "lily"=>array("name"=>"Lily Bernard", "sex"=>"F", "age"=>37),
   "ayesha"=>array("name"=>"Ayesha Siddika", "sex"=>"F", "age"=>26),
   "afif"=>array("name"=>"Afif", "sex"=>"M", "age"=>2)
);
class MyRecursiveIterator extends ArrayIterator implements
                                           RecursiveIterator
{
  public function hasChildren()
  {
    return is_array($this->current());
  }
  public function getChildren()
  {
    return new MyRecursiveIterator($this->current());
  }
}
$persons = new ArrayObject($arr);
$MRI = new RecursiveIteratorIterator(new MyRecursiveIterator($persons
));
foreach ($MRI as $key=>$person)
echo $key." : ".$person."\n";
?>
```

The output is:

```
name  : John Abraham
sex  : M
age  : 27
name  : Lily Bernard
sex  : F
age  : 37
name  : Ayesha Siddika
sex  : F
age  : 26
name  : Afif
sex  : M
age  : 2
```

SPLFileObject

This is another fantastic object introduced in SPL for basic file operations. You can iterate through the content of the file in a more elegant way using this object. In `SPLFileObject`, the following methods are supported:

```
Array
(
        [0]  => __construct
        [1]  => getFilename
        [2]  => rewind
        [3]  => eof
        [4]  => valid
        [5]  => fgets
        [6]  => fgetcsv
        [7]  => flock
        [8]  => fflush
        [9]  => ftell
        [10] => fseek
        [11] => fgetc
        [12] => fpassthru
        [13] => fgetss
        [14] => fscanf
        [15] => fwrite
        [16] => fstat
        [17] => ftruncate
        [18] => current
        [19] => key
        [20] => next
        [21] => setFlags
        [22] => getFlags
        [23] => setMaxLineLen
        [24] => getMaxLineLen
        [25] => hasChildren
        [26] => getChildren
        [27] => seek
        [28] => getCurrentLine
        [29] => __toString
)
```

If you carefully look into it, you will find that general file functions in PHP are implemented in this object, which gives you more flexibility to work with.

In the following example we will discuss how to use `SPLFileObject`:

```
<?
$file = new SplFileObject("c:\\lines.txt");
foreach( $file as $line ) {
    echo $line;
}
?>
```

Therefore, it works in the same was as an Iterator, you can rewind, seek, and perform other general tasks. There are also some interesting functions like getMaxLineLen, fstat, hasChildren, getChildren etc.

Using `SPLFileObject` you can retrieve remote files too.

SPLFileInfo

This is another object introduced by SPL, which helps you to retrieve file information of any specific file. Let's have a look at the structure first:

```
Array
(
    [0]  => __construct
    [1]  => getPath
    [2]  => getFilename
    [3]  => getPathname
    [4]  => getPerms
    [5]  => getInode
    [6]  => getSize
    [7]  => getOwner
    [8]  => getGroup
    [9]  => getATime
    [10] => getMTime
    [11] => getCTime
    [12] => getType
    [13] => isWritable
    [14] => isReadable
    [15] => isExecutable
    [16] => isFile
    [17] => isDir
    [18] => isLink
    [19] => getFileInfo
    [20] => getPathInfo
    [21] => openFile
```

```
    [22] => setFileClass
    [23] => setInfoClass
    [24] => __toString
)
```

You can use SPLFileInfo to open any file. However, what is more interesting is that it supports overloading the opening of a file. You can supply your open file manager class to it and it will be invoked while opening a file.

Let's take a look at the following example.

```php
<?php
class CustomFO extends SplFileObject
{
  private $i=1;
  public function current()
  {
    return $this->i++ . ":    " .
            htmlspecialchars($this->getCurrentLine())."";
  }
}
$SFI= new SplFileInfo( "splfileinfo2.php" );
$SFI->setFileClass( "CustomFO" );
$file = $SFI->openFile(  );
echo "<pre>";
foreach( $file as $line )
{
  echo $line;
}
?>
```

This example will output the following:

```
1:
2:    <?php
3:
4:    class CustomFO extends SplFileObject
      {
5:      private $i=1;
6:      public function current()
      {
7:
8:        return $this->i++ . ":    " .
              htmlspecialchars($this->getCurrentLine())."";
9:      }
```

```
10:     }
11:     $SFI= new SplFileInfo( "splfileinfo2.php" );
12:
13:     $SFI->setFileClass( "CustomFO" );
14:     $file = $SFI->openFile(   );
15:     echo "<pre>";
16:     foreach( $file as $line )
        {
17:         echo $line;
18:     }
19:
20:     ?>
21:
22:
```

SPLObjectStorage

Beside Directory, File Objects and Iterators, SPL also introduced another cool
object which can store any object inside it with special facilities. This object is called
SPLObjectStorage. We will understand this using the example later on in this chapter.

SPLObjectStorage can store any object in it. When you change the main object, the
object that is stored inside the SPLObjectStorage will also be changed. If you try to
add a specific object more than once, it won't add actually. You can also delete the
object from the storage any time.

Besides this, SPLObjectStorage provides the facility to iterate through a collection
of stored objects. Let's take a look at the following example, which demonstrates the
use of SPLObjectStorage:

```php
<?
$os = new SplObjectStorage();
$person = new stdClass();// a standard object
$person->name = "Its not a name";
$person->age = "100";
$os->attach($person); //attached in the storage
foreach ($os as $object)
{
  print_r($object);
  echo "\n";
}
$person->name = "New Name"; //change the name
echo str_repeat("-",30)."\n"; //just a format code
```

```
foreach ($os as $object)
{
  print_r($object); //you see that it changes the original object
  echo "\n";
}
$person2 = new stdClass();
$person2->name = "Another Person";
$person2->age = "80";
$os->attach($person2);
echo str_repeat("-",30)."\n";
foreach ($os as $object)
{
  print_r($object);
  echo "\n";
}
echo "\n".$os->contains($person);//seek
$os->rewind();
echo "\n".$os->current()->name;
$os->detach($person); //remove the object from collection
echo "\n".str_repeat("-",30)."\n";
foreach ($os as $object)
{
  print_r($object);
  echo "\n";
}
?>
```

The output is as follows:

```
stdClass Object
(
  [name] => It's not a name
  [age] => 100
)

------------------------------
stdClass Object
(
  [name] => New Name
  [age] => 100
)

------------------------------
stdClass Object
```

```
(
   [name] => New Name
   [age] => 100
)
stdClass Object
(
   [name] => Another Person
   [age] => 80
)
1
New Name
- - - - - - - - - - - - - - - - - - - - - - - - - - -
stdClass Object
(
   [name] => Another Person
   [age] => 80
)
```

Summary

After introducing PHP5 to the world, the PHP team introduced the strong object oriented programming in PHP to PHP developers. PHP5 comes with a lot of handy built-in objects amongst which SPL is a fantastic one. It eases programming for many tasks, which were once quite tough. So SPL introduced many objects that we have just discussed and learned how to use. As the PHP manual doesn't have updated and detailed information on all of these classes, you can count this chapter as a good reference for programming with SPL objects.

- Ability to create compressed connections
- Ability to connect over SSL
- Support for Prepared Statements
- Support for Stored Procedure (SP)
- Support for better replication and transaction

We will look into some of these features in the following examples. But of course we are not going for anything introductory to MySQL, because that is out of scope for this book. We will just show you how to use OO interface using MySQLi and how to use some of these advanced features.

Connecting to MySQL in an OO Way

Remember those old days when you had to use procedural function `call` to connect to MySQL, even from your objects. Those days are over. Now you can take advantage of complete OO interface of MySQLi to talk to MySQL (well, there are a few procedural methods, but overall it's completely OO). Take a look at the following example:

```
<?
$mysqli = new mysqli("localhost", "user", "password", "dbname");
if (mysqli_connect_errno()) {
   echo("Failed to connect, the error message is : ".
                                      mysqli_connect_error());
   exit();
}
?>
```

If the connection fails, you may get an error message like this:

```
Failed to connect, the error message is : Access denied for user
                  'my_user'@'localhost' (using password: YES)
```

Selecting Data in an OO Way

Let's see how to select data from a table in an OO way using MySQLi API.

```
<?php
$mysqli = new mysqli("localhost", "un" "pwd", "db");
if (mysqli_connect_errno()) {
   echo("Failed to connect, the error message is : ".
                                      mysqli_connect_error());
   exit();
```

```
}
/* close connection */
$result = $mysqli ->query("select * from users");
while ($data = $result->fetch_object())
{
   echo $data->name." : '".$data->pass."' \n";
}
?>
```

The output is as following:

```
robin : 'no password'
tipu : 'bolajabena'
```

 Please note that it is not good practice to store users' passwords in plain text in your database without encrypting them in some way. The best way is to store just the hash of their passwords using some hash routines like md5()

Updating Data in an OO Way

There is no special deal with it. You can update your data as you previously did with MySQL extension. But for the sake of OO style, we are showing an example of how you can do that with `mysqli_query()` function as shown in the above example. Instantiate an instance of MySQLi object and then run the query.

Prepared Statements

Here we are in a really interesting section which has been introduced for the first time in PHP OO using MySQLi extension. The prepared statements are introduced in MySQL 5.0 versions (dynamic SQL) for better security and flexibility. It has a great performance boost over the regular one.

So what is actually a prepared statement? A prepared statement is nothing but a regular query that is pre-compiled by the MySQL sever that could be invoked later. Prepared statements reduce the chances of SQL injection and offers greater performance over the general non-prepared queries, as it need not perform different compilation steps at the run time.(It is already compiled, remember?)

The following are advantages of using prepared statements:

- Better Performance
- Prevention of SQL injection
- Saving memory while handling blobs

But there are drawbacks too!

- There is no performance boost if you use prepared statements for a single call.
- There is no query cache for using prepared statements.
- Chance of memory leak if statements are not closed explicitly.
- Not all statements can be used as a prepared statement.

Prepared statements can accept parameters at run time in the same order you specify them whilst preparing the query. In this section we will learn about creating prepared statements, passing values to them, and fetching results.

Basic Prepared Statements

Let's prepare a statement using PHP's native MySQLi extension. In the following example we will make a prepared statement, execute it, and fetch the result from it:

```
<?
$mysqli  = new mysqli("localhost", "un" "pwd", "db");
if (mysqli_connect_errno()) {
   echo("Failed to connect, the error message is : ".
                              mysqli_connect_error());
   exit();
}
$stmt = $mysqli ->prepare("select name, pass from users
                                       order by name");
$stmt->execute();
//$name=null;
$stmt->bind_result($name, $pass);
while ($stmt->fetch())
{
   echo $name."<br/>";
}
?>
```

So what did we actually do in the above example?

1. We prepared the statement using the following code:

```
$stmt = $mysqli->prepare("select name, pass from users order
                                        by name");
```

2. Then we executed it:

   ```
   $stmt->execute();
   ```

3. Then we bound two variables with it, as there are two variables in our query:

   ```
   $stmt->bind_result($name, $pass);
   ```

4. Finally we fetched the result using:

   ```
   $stmt->fetch()
   ```

Whenever we called `fetch()`, the bound variables are populated with values. So we can now use them.

Prepared Statements with Variables

The advantage of prepared statements is that you can use variables with queries. First you can prepare the query by placing a ? sign at the appropriate place, and then you can pass the value after preparing it. Let's have a look at the following example:

```
<?
$mysqli = new mysqli("localhost", "un" "pwd", "db");
if (mysqli_connect_errno()) {
   echo("Failed to connect, the error message is : ".
                                   mysqli_connect_error());
   exit();
}
$stmt = $mysqli->prepare("select name, pass from users
                                      where name=?");
$stmt->bind_param("s",$name); //binding name as string
$name = "tipu";
$stmt->execute();
$name=null;
$stmt->bind_result($name, $pass);

while ($r = $stmt->fetch())
{
   echo $pass."<br/>";
}
?>
```

Here we prepare the query `"select name, pass from users where name=?"` where the name is definitely a string type value. As we bind parameters in the previous example for the result using `bind_results()`, here we have to bind parameters using `bind_params()` function. Besides that, we need to supply the data type of the parameters bound.

MySQL prepared statements support four types of parameters:

- i, means the corresponding variable has type integer
- d, means the corresponding variable has type double
- s, means the corresponding variable has type string
- b, means the corresponding variable is a blob and will be sent in packets

As our parameter is a string, we used the following line to bind the parameter:

```
$stmt->bind_param("s",$name);
```

After binding the variable, now we set the value to $name and call the execute() function. After that we fetch the values as before.

Using BLOB with Prepared Statements

Prepared statements support handling **BLOB** or **Binary Large Objects** efficiently. If you manage BLOB with prepared statements, it will save you from greater memory consumption by sending the data as packets. Let's see how we can store BLOB (in this case, an image file).

Prepared statements support sending data in chunks using the send_long_data() function. In the following example we will store the image using this function, though you can send them as usual, unless your data exceeds the limit defined by the max_allowed_packet MySQL configuration variable.

```
<?
$mysqli = new mysqli("localhost", "un" "pwd", "db");
if (mysqli_connect_errno()) {
   echo("Failed to connect, the error message is : ".
                           mysqli_connect_error());
   exit();
}
$stmt = $mysqli->prepare("insert into images value(NULL,?)");
$stmt->bind_param("b",$image);
$image = file_get_contents("signature.jpg");//fetching content of
//a file
$stmt->send_long_data(0,$image);
$stmt->execute();
?>
```

Our table schema is as shown below:

```
CREATE TABLE 'images' (
  'id' int(11) NOT NULL auto_increment,
  'image' mediumblob,
  PRIMARY KEY  ('id')
) ENGINE=MyISAM;
```

We choose medium BLOB as our data type because blob can store only 65KB of data, where as medium BLOB can store more than 16MB, and long blob can store more than 4GB data in it.

Now we will restore this BLOB data using the image again in prepared statement:

```php
<?
$mysqli = new mysqli("localhost", "username", "password", "test");
if (mysqli_connect_errno()) {
    echo("Failed to connect, the error message is : ".
                                        mysqli_connect_error());
    exit();
}
$stmt = $mysqli->prepare("select image from images where id=?");
$stmt->bind_param("i",$id);
$id = $_GET['id'];
$stmt->execute();
$image=NULL;
$stmt->bind_result($image);
$stmt->fetch();
header("Content-type: image/jpeg");
echo $image;
?>
```

Executing Stored Procedure with MySQLi and PHP

Stored procedure is another new addition to MySQL 5 which reduces the need for client-side queries to a great extent. Using MySQLi extension, you can execute stored procedures in MySQL. We are not going to discuss stored procedures as that is out of scope for this book. There are several articles available in the Internet that will help you in writing stored procedures in MySQL. You can read this awesome one for getting a basic idea about advanced MySQL features: http://dev.mysql.com/tech-resources/articles/mysql-storedprocedures.pdf

Let's create a small stored procedure and run it using PHP. This stored procedure can take an input and insert that record in a table:

```
DELIMITER $$;
DROP PROCEDURE IF EXISTS 'test'.'sp_create_user'$$
CREATE PROCEDURE 'sp_create_user'(IN uname VARCHAR(50))
BEGIN
INSERT INTO users(id,name) VALUES (null, uname);
END$$
DELIMITER ;$$
```

If you run this stored procedure in your database (using MySQL query builder or anything) the `sp_create_user` procedure will be created.

 You can manually execute any stored, procedure from MySQL client using "Execute" command. For example to execute the above stored procedure you have to use `call sp_create_user('`*username*`')`.

Now we will run this stored procedure using PHP code. Let's see.

```
<?
$mysqli = new mysqli("localhost", "username", "password", "test");
if (mysqli_connect_errno()) {
    echo("Failed to connect, the error message is : ".
                            mysqli_connect_error());
    exit();
}

$mysqli->query("call sp_create_user('hasin')");
?>
```

That's it!

PDO

Another new extension added in PHP 5.1 for managing databases is PDO (although PDO was available with PHP 5.0 as a PECL Extension). This comes with a set of drivers for working with different database engines. **PDO** stands for **PHP Data Objects**. It is developed to provide a lightweight interface for different database engines. And one of the very good features of PDO is that it works like a Data Access Layer so that you can use the same function names for all database engines.

You can connect to different databases using DSN (Data Source Name) strings. In the following example we will connect to a MySQL databases and retrieve some data.

```php
<?php
$dsn = 'mysql:dbname=test;host=localhost;';
$user = 'user';
$password = 'password';
try {
    $pdo = new PDO($dsn, $user, $password);
}
catch (PDOException $e)
{
    echo 'Connection failed: ' . $e->getMessage();
}
$result = $pdo->query("select * from users");
foreach ($result as $row)
echo $row['name'];
?>
```

That's fairly hassle free, right? It just connects to MySQL server with the DSN (here it connects to test database) and then executes the query. And Finally we display the result.

So what would this be like if we connected to a SQLite database?

```php
<?php
$dsn = 'sqlite:abcd.db';
try
{
    $pdo = new PDO($dsn);
    $pdo->exec("CREATE TABLE users (id int, name VARCHAR)");
    $pdo->exec("DELETE FROM users");
    $pdo->exec("INSERT INTO users (name) VALUES('afif')");
    $pdo->exec("INSERT INTO users (name) VALUES('tipu')");
    $pdo->exec("INSERT INTO users (name) VALUES('robin')");
}
catch (PDOException $e) {
    echo 'Connection failed: ' . $e->getMessage();
}
$result = $pdo->query("select * from users");
foreach ($result as $row)
echo $row['name'];
?>
```

See there is no change in the code except the DSN.

You can also create a SQLite database in memory and perform the operation there. Let's see the following code:

```php
<?php
$dsn = 'sqlite::memory:';
try {
    $pdo = new PDO($dsn);
    $pdo->exec("CREATE TABLE users (id int, name VARCHAR)");
    $pdo->exec("DELETE FROM users");
    $pdo->exec("INSERT INTO users (name) VALUES('afif')");
    $pdo->exec("INSERT INTO users (name) VALUES('tipu')");
    $pdo->exec("INSERT INTO users (name) VALUES('robin')");
}
catch (PDOException $e)
{
    echo 'Connection failed: ' . $e->getMessage();
}

$result = $pdo->query("select * from users");
foreach ($result as $row)
echo $row['name'];

?>
```

We just changed the DSN here.

DSN Settings for Different Databases Engines

Let us take a look at the DSN settings for different database engines to connect with PDO. Supported database drivers are as shown below:

- PDO_DBLIB for FreeTDS/Microsoft SQL Server/Sybase
- PDO_FIREBIRD for Firebird/Interbase 6
- PDO_INFORMIX for IBM Informix Dynamic Server
- PDO_MYSQL for MySQL 3.x/4.x/5.x
- PDO_OCI for Oracle Call Interface
- PDO_ODBC for ODBC v3 (IBM DB2, unixODBC and win32 ODBC)
- PDO_PGSQL for PostgreSQL
- PDO_SQLITE for SQLite 3 and SQLite 2

Let's have a look at these sample driver-specific DSN settings:

```
mssql:host=localhost;dbname=testdb
sybase:host=localhost;dbname=testdb
dblib:host=localhost;dbname=testdb
firebird:User=john;Password=mypass;Database=DATABASE.GDE;
                        DataSource=localhost;Port=3050
informix:host=host.domain.com; service=9800;database=common_db;
    server=ids_server; protocol=onsoctcp;EnableScrollableCursors=1
mysql:host=localhost;port=3307;dbname=testdb
mysql:unix_socket=/tmp/mysql.sock;dbname=testdb
oci:mydb
oci:dbname=//localhost:1521/mydb
odbc:testdb
odbc:DRIVER={IBM DB2 ODBC
 DRIVER};HOSTNAME=localhost;PORT=50000;DATABASE=SAMPLE;PROTOCOL=TCPIP;
                        UID=db2inst1;PWD=ibmdb2;
odbc:Driver={Microsoft Access Driver
                (*.mdb)};Dbq=C:\\db.mdb;Uid=Admin
pgsql:dbname=example;user=nobody;password=change_me;host=localhost;
                        port=5432
sqlite:/opt/databases/mydb.sq3
sqlite::memory:
sqlite2:/opt/databases/mydb.sq2
sqlite2::memory:
```

Using Prepared Statements with PDO

Using PDO you can run prepared statements against your database. The benefits are the same as before. It increases the performance for multiple calls by parsing and caching the server-side query and it also eliminates the chance of SQL injection.

PDO prepared statements can take named variables, unlike what we've seen in the examples of MySQLi.

Let's take a look at the following example to understand this:

```php
<?php
$dsn = 'mysql:dbname=test;host=localhost;';
$user = 'username';
$password = 'password';
try {
    $pdo = new PDO($dsn, $user, $password);
```

```
    } catch (PDOException $e)
    {
        echo 'Connection failed: ' . $e->getMessage();
    }
    $stmt = $pdo->prepare("select id from users where name=:name");
    $name = "tipu";
    $stmt->bindParam(":name",$name, PDO::PARAM_STR);
    $stmt->execute();

    $stmt->bindColumn("id",$id);
    $stmt->fetch();
    echo $id;
    ?>
```

But you can also run the example like this:

```
<?php
$dsn = 'mysql:dbname=test;host=localhost;';
$user = 'username';
$password = 'password';
try {
    $pdo = new PDO($dsn, $user, $password);
}
catch (PDOException $e)
{
    echo 'Connection failed: ' . $e->getMessage();
}
$stmt = $pdo->prepare("select id from users where name=?");
$name = "tipu";
$stmt->bindParam(1,$name, PDO::PARAM_STR);
$stmt->execute();
$stmt->bindColumn("id",$id);
$stmt->fetch();
echo $id;
?>
```

Instead of calling `bindParam()`, you can use `bindValues()` like the following one:

```
$stmt->bindValue(1,"tipu", PDO::PARAM_STR);
```

Calling Stored Procedures

PDO provides an easy way to call stored procedures. All you have to do is run "CALL SPNAME(PARAMS)" via `exec()` method:

```
$pdo->exec("CALL sp_create_user('david')");
```

Other Interesting Functions

There are several other interesting functions available in PDO. For example, take a look at the list below:

- `fetchAll()`
- `fetchColumn()`
- `rowCount()`
- `setFetchMode()`

The `fetchAll()` function can fetch all records from a result set. Let's have a look at the following example:

```
$stmt = $pdo->prepare("select * from users");
$stmt->execute();
echo "<pre>";
print_r($stmt->fetchAll());
echo "</pre>";
```

The `fetchColumn()` function helps to select data from any specific column after executing the statement. Let's take a look:

```
$stmt = $pdo->prepare("select * from users");
$stmt->execute();
while ($name = $stmt->fetchColumn(1))
{
   echo $name."<br/>";
}
```

`rowCount()` returns the number of affected rows after performing any UPDATE or DELETE query. But you must remember that it returns the number of affected rows by the latest executed query.

```
$stmt = $pdo->prepare("DELETE from users WHERE name='Anonymous'");
$stmt->execute();
echo $stmt->rowCount();
```

`setFetchMode()` helps you to set the fetch mode of PDO prepared statements. The available values are:

- `PDO::FETCH_NUM`: Fetch results as a numerically indexed array
- `PDO::FETCH_ASSOC`: Fetch rows as index by column names as keys
- `PDO::FETCH_BOTH`: Fetch as both of the above
- `PDO::FETCH_OBJ`: Fetch the rows as objects where column names are set as properties.

Introduction to Data Abstraction Layers

Data Abstraction Layers (DALs) are developed to provide unified interfaces to work with every database engine. It provides similar API to work with every database engine independently. As the function names are similar for all platforms, they are easier to work with, easier to remember, and of course make your code portable. To make you understand the necessity of DAL, let me explain a common scenario.

Suppose Team Y gets a big project. Their client says that they will use MySQL. So team Y develops the application and when the time comes to deliver, the client requests the team to give support for PostgreSQL. They will pay for this change but they require the change early.

Team Y had designed the application using all native MySQL functions. So what will Team Y do? Will they rewrite everything to give support for PostgreSQL? Well, that is the only way they have to. But what will happen if they need to give support for MSSQL in the near future? Another rewrite? Can you imagine the cost of refactoring each and every time?

To save from these disasters, here comes the need for DAL where the code will remain the same and it could be changed to support any DB at any time without any major change.

There are many popular libraries to implement DAL for PHP. To name some of those, ADOdb and PEAR::MDB2 are very popular. PEAR::DB was very popular but its development has been discontinued (`http://blog.agoraproduction.com/index.php?/archives/42-PEARDB-is-DEPRECATED,-GOT-IT.html#extended`).

In this section we will discuss PEAR::MDB2 and ADOdb. We will see the basic database operations using it and learn how to install these libraries for working around.

ADOdb

ADOdb is a nice and popular data abstraction layer developed by John Lim and released under LGPL. This is one of the very best data abstraction layers for PHP. You can get the latest version of ADOdb from `http://adodb.sourceforge.net`.

Installing ADOdb

There is no install of ADodb as such. It is a set of classes and regular scripts. So all you have to do is just extract the archive in a location from where you can include the script. Let's take a look at the following image to understand the directory structure after extracting:

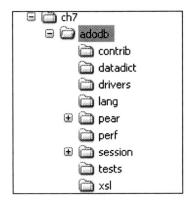

Connecting to Different Databases

Like PDO, you can connect to different database drivers using ADOdb. DSN is different from PDO. Let's take a look at the supported database list and their DSN strings.

ADOdb supports a common DSN format, like this:

```
$driver://$username:$password@hostname/$database?options[=value]
```

So what are the available drivers supported by ADOdb? Let's take a look below. This is a list taken from the ADOdb manual for your understanding:

Name	Tested	Database	Prerequisites	Operating Systems
access	B	Microsoft Access/Jet. You need to create an ODBC DSN.	ODBC	Windows only
ado	B	Generic ADO, not tuned for specific databases. Allows DSN-less connections. For best performance, use an OLEDB provider. This is the base class for all ado drivers. You can set $db->codePage before connecting.	ADO or OLEDB provider	Windows only
ado_access	B	Microsoft Access/Jet using ADO. Allows DSN-less connections. For best performance, use an OLEDB provider.	ADO or OLEDB provider	Windows only

Name	Tested	Database	Prerequisites	Operating Systems
ado_mssql	B	Microsoft SQL Server using ADO. Allows DSN-less connections. For best performance, use an OLEDB provider.	ADO or OLEDB provider	Windows only
db2	C	Uses PHP's db2-specific extension for better performance.	DB2 CLI/ODBC interface	Unix and Windows. Requires IBM DB2 Universal Database client
odbc_db2	C	Connects to DB2 using generic ODBC extension.	DB2 CLI/ODBC interface	Unix and Windows. Unix install hints. I have had reports that the `$host` and `$database` params have to be reversed in `Connect()` when using the CLI interface
vfp	A	Microsoft Visual FoxPro. You need to create an ODBC DSN.	ODBC	Windows only
fbsql	C	FrontBase.	?	Unix and Windows
ibase	B	Interbase 6 or earlier. Some users report you might need to use this `$db->PConnect('localhost:c:/ibase/employee.gdb', "sysdba", "masterkey")` to connect. Lacks `Affected_Rows` currently. You can set `$db->role`, `$db->dialect`, `$db->buffers` and `$db->charSet` before connecting.	Interbase client	Unix and Windows
firebird	B	Firebird version of interbase.	Interbase client	Unix and Windows
borland_ibase	C	Borland version of Interbase 6.5 or later. Very sad that the forks differ.	Interbase client	Unix and Windows

Name	Tested	Database	Prerequisites	Operating Systems
informix	C	Generic informix driver. Use this if you are using Informix 7.3 or later.	Informix client	Unix and Windows
informix72	C	Informix databases before Informix 7.3 that do no support `SELECT FIRST`.	Informix client	Unix and Windows
ldap	C	LDAP driver. See this example for usage information.	LDAP extension	?
mssql	A	Microsoft SQL Server 7 and later. Works with Microsoft SQL Server 2000 also. Note that date formating is problematic with this driver. For example, the PHP MSSQL extension does not return the seconds for datetime!	Mssql client	Unix and Windows. Unix install howto and another one.
mssqlpo	A	Portable mssql driver. Identical to above mssql driver, except that '||', the concatenation operator, is converted to '+'. Useful for porting scripts from most other sql variants that use ||.	Mssql client	Unix and Windows. Unix install howto.
mysql	A	MySQL without transaction support. You can also set `$db->clientFlags` before connecting.	MySQL client	Unix and Windows
mysqli	B	Supports the newer PHP5 MySQL API.	MySQL 4.1+ client	Unix and Windows
mysqlt or maxsql	A	MySQL with transaction support. We recommend using || as the concat operator for best portability. This can be done by running MySQL using: `mysqld --ansi or mysqld --sql-mode=PIPES_AS_CONCAT`	MySQL client	Unix and Windows
oci8	A	Oracle 8/9. Has more functionality than oracle driver (eg. `Affected_Rows`). You might have to `putenv('ORACLE_HOME=...')` before Connect/PConnect. There are 2 ways of connecting: with server IP and service name: `PConnect('serverip:1521','scott','tiger','service')` or using an entry in TNSNAMES.ORA or ONAMES or HOSTNAMES: `PConnect(false, 'scott', 'tiger', $oraname)`. Since 2.31, we support Oracle REF cursor variables directly (see `ExecuteCursor`).	Oracle client	Unix and Windows

Name	Tested	Database	Prerequisites	Operating Systems
oci805	C	Supports reduced Oracle functionality for Oracle 8.0.5. `SelectLimit` is not as efficient as in the oci8 or oci8po drivers.	Oracle client	Unix and Windows
oci8po	A	Oracle 8/9 portable driver. This is nearly identical with the oci8 driver except (a) bind variables in `Prepare()` use the ? convention, instead of `:bindvar`, (b) field names use the more common PHP convention of lowercase names. Use this driver if porting from other databases is important. Otherwise the oci8 driver offers better performance.	Oracle client	Unix and Windows
odbc	A	Generic ODBC, not tuned for specific databases. To connect, use `PConnect('DSN','user','pwd')`. This is the base class for all ODBC derived drivers.	ODBC	Unix and Windows. Unix hints
odbc_mssql	A	Uses ODBC to connect to MSSQL	ODBC	Unix and Windows
odbc_oracle	C	Uses ODBC to connect to Oracle	ODBC	Unix and Windows
odbtp	B	Generic odbtp driver. Odbtp is a software for accessing Windows ODBC data sources from other operating systems.	odbtp	Unix and Windows
odbtp_ unicode	C	Odtbp with unicode support	odbtp	Unix and Windows
oracle	C	Implements old Oracle 7 client API. Use oci8 driver if possible for better performance.	Oracle client	Unix and Windows
netezza	C	Netezza driver. Netezza is based on PostGREs code-base.	?	?
pdo	C	Generic PDO driver for PHP5.	PDO extension and database specific drivers	Unix and Windows
postgres	A	Generic PostgreSQL driver. Currently identical to postgres7 driver.	PostgreSQL client	Unix and Windows
postgres64	A	For PostgreSQL 6.4 and earlier which does not support LIMIT internally.	PostgreSQL client	Unix and Windows
postgres7	A	PostgreSQL which supports LIMIT and other version 7 functionality.	PostgreSQL client	Unix and Windows

Name	Tested	Database	Prerequisites	Operating Systems
postgres8	A	Currently identical to postgres7.	PostgreSQL client	Unix and Windows
sapdb	C	SAP DB. Should work reliably as based on ODBC driver.	SAP ODBC client	?
sqlanywhere	C	Sybase SQL Anywhere. Should work reliably as based on ODBC driver.	SQL Anywhere ODBC client	?
sqlite	B	SQLite.	-	Unix and Windows
sqlitepo	B	Portable SQLite driver. This is because assoc mode does not work like other drivers in SQLite. Namely, when selecting (joining) multiple tables, the table names are included in the assoc keys in the "sqlite" driver. In "sqlitepo" driver, the table names are stripped from the returned column names. When this results in a conflict, the first field get preference.	-	Unix and Windows
sybase	C	Sybase.	Sybase client	Unix and Windows

Basic Database Operations using ADOdb

Remember the directory structure that saw minutes ago? Now we are going to make use of those scripts. In this section we will learn basic database operation using ADOdb. Let's connect to MySQL and perform a basic operation:

```
<?
include("adodb/adodb.inc.php");
$dsn = 'mysql://username:password@localhost/test?persist';
$conn = ADONewConnection($dsn);
$conn->setFetchMode(ADODB_FETCH_ASSOC);
$recordSet = $conn->Execute('select * from users');
if (!$recordSet)
print $conn->ErrorMsg(); //if any error is there
else
while (!$recordSet->EOF) {
  echo $recordSet->fields['name'].'<BR>';
  $recordSet->MoveNext();
}
?>
```

Let's see an alternate connection example:

```
<?
include("adodb/adodb.inc.php");
$conn =ADONewConnection('mysql');//just the RDBMS type
$conn->connect("localhost","username","password","test");
//here comes the credentials
?>
```

Inserting, Deleting, and Updating Records

You can execute any SQL statement using `execute()` method of `ADONewConnection` or `ADOConnection` object. So nothing is new here. But let's see how can we insert/delete/update some records and track the success or failure.

```
<?
include("adodb/adodb.inc.php");
$conn =ADONewConnection('mysql');
$conn->connect("localhost","user","password","test");
$conn->setFetchMode(ADODB_FETCH_ASSOC);
$res = $conn->execute("insert into users(name) values('test')");
echo $conn->Affected_Rows();
?>
```

So, `Affected_Rows` gives you the result for these scenarios.

Insert Id

If you are looking to find the latest inserted ID, you can use the `Insert_Id()` function.

Executing Prepared Statements

ADOdb provides easy API to create and execute prepared statements. Let's take a look at the following example to understand how that works:

```
<?
include("adodb/adodb.inc.php");
$conn =ADONewConnection('mysql');
$conn->connect("localhost","user","password","test")  ;
$conn->setFetchMode(ADODB_FETCH_ASSOC);
$stmt = $conn->Prepare('insert into users(name) values (?)');
$conn->Execute($stmt,array((string) "afif"));
echo $conn->Affected_Rows();
?>
```

You can retrieve records in the same way.

MDB2

MDB2 is another popular data abstraction library developed under PEAR by combining the best features of PEAR::DB and Metabase. It provides very consistent API, improved performance, and solid development platform over DB and MDB. MDB2 comes with an excellent set of documentation. In this chapter we surely cannot cover all the features supported by MDB2 but we will go through the basic features to make you understand how it works.

Installing MDB2

Installing MDB2 requires a working version of PEAR. So to work with MDB2 you must have PEAR installed and functioning in your machine. If you don't have PEAR installed, the following tip will be helpful for you.

Installing PEAR

Go to `http://pear.php.net/go-pear` and save the page as `go-pear.php` in your hard drive. Now apply the command `php /path/to/go-pear.php` in your shell or command prompt and follow the instructions there. If it asks whether you want to install MDB2, say 'Yes'. Also say Yes, if it wants to modify your `php.ini` file. Don't worry, it will just add entries to make PEAR available in your current include path, and all other settings will remain the same as before. So you are done.

If you have PEAR I installed but not MDB2, then you can install it in a second. Open your shell or command prompt and apply the following commands:

```
pear install MDB2
pear install MDB2_Driver_$driver
```

Where `$driver` could be anything like SQLite, PgSQL, MySQL, MYSQLi, oci8, MSSQL, and ibase. So for example, to install MySQL driver you have to apply the command:

```
pear install MDB2_Driver_mysql
```

That's it. You are done.

Connecting to Database

Using MDB2 you can connect to different database engines. MDB2 also has a formatted DSN string to connect. The format of that DSN is as shown:

```
phptype(dbsyntax)://username:password@protocol+hostspec/database?
                                                    option=value
```

But there are some variations in this DSN. These are listed here:

```
phptype://username:password@protocol+hostspec:110//usr/db_file.db
phptype://username:password@hostspec/database
phptype://username:password@hostspec
phptype://username@hostspec
phptype://hostspec/database
phptype://hostspec
phptype:///database
phptype:///database?option=value&anotheroption=anothervalue
```

The supported drivers (PHPtype) are shown here:

```
fbsql   -> FrontBase
ibase   -> InterBase / Firebird (requires PHP 5)
mssql   -> Microsoft SQL Server (NOT for Sybase. Compile PHP --with-
                                                            mssql)
mysql   -> MySQL
mysqli  -> MySQL (supports new authentication protocol) (requires
                                                        PHP 5)
oci8    -> Oracle 7/8/9/10
pgsql   -> PostgreSQL
querysim -> QuerySim
sqlite  -> SQLite 2
```

Now let's connect to MySQL:

```php
<?php
set_include_path(get_include_path().";".
                    "C:/Program Files/PHP/pear;");
require_once 'MDB2.php';
$dsn = 'mysql://user:password@localhost/test';
$options = array('persistent' => true
);
$mdb2 = MDB2::factory($dsn, $options);
if (PEAR::isError($mdb2)) {
    die($mdb2->getMessage());
```

```
}
// ...
$result = $mdb2->query("select * from users");
while ($row = $result->fetchRow(MDB2_FETCHMODE_ASSOC))
{
    echo $row['name']."\n";
}
$mdb2->disconnect();
?>
```

Executing Prepared Statements

You can execute prepared statements using MDB2 easily. MDB2 provides flexible API for creating and executing prepared statements. In the following example we will execute two types of prepared statements. One which will just execute some insert/update/delete queries, and another which will return some data as output.

```php
<?php
set_include_path(get_include_path().";".
                        "C:/Program Files/PHP/pear;");
require_once 'MDB2.php';
$dsn = 'mysql://user:password@localhost/test';
$options = array('persistent' => true
);
$mdb2 = MDB2::factory($dsn, $options);
if (PEAR::isError($mdb2)) {
    die($mdb2->getMessage());
}
$stmt = $mdb2->Prepare("insert into users(name)
                values(?)",array("text"),MDB2_PREPARE_MANIP);
//for DML statements, we should use MDB2_PREPARE_MANIP and For
//Reading we should use MDB2_PREPARE_RESULT
echo $stmt->execute("Mohiuddin");
$stmt = $mdb2->Prepare("select name from users where
                    id=?",array("integer"),array("text"));
$result = $stmt->execute(11);
if (PEAR::isError($result))
echo $result->getMessage();
while ($row = $result->fetchRow())
{
  echo $row[0];
}
?>
```

Now what if we want to insert in multiple fields? Well for example, if we have another field like "age" in our table, we need to pass data like this:

```
$stmt = $mdb2->Prepare("insert into users(name,age)
    values(?)",array("text","integer"),MDB2_PREPARE_MANIP);
echo $stmt->execute("Mohiuddin",2);
```

Or:

```
$stmt = $mdb2->Prepare("insert into users(name,age)
    values(?)",array("text","integer"),MDB2_PREPARE_MANIP);
echo $stmt->execute(array("Mohiuddin",2));
```

So we can also insert multiple rows at once using `executeMultiple()` method:

```
$stmt = $mdb2->Prepare("insert into users(name,age) values(?)",
            array("text","integer"),MDB2_PREPARE_MANIP);
echo $stmt->executeMultiple(array(array("Mohiuddin",2),
                                    array("another",3));
```

That's it.

Introduction to ActiveRecord

ActiveRecord is a design pattern created to solve the data accessing problem in a fairly readable manner. Using ActiveRecord design pattern you can manipulate data like a charm. In this section we will go through the basic features of an ActiveRecord implementation in PHP.

Let's see how ActiveRecord actually works. For this, we will use ADOdb's active record implementation. Adodb provides a class named `Adodb_Active_Record` devoted to it.

Let's create a table in our database with the following structure:

```
CREATE TABLE 'users' (
  'id' int(11) NOT NULL auto_increment,
  'name' varchar(250),
  'pass' varchar(32),
  PRIMARY KEY ('id')
) ENGINE=MyISAM;
```

Creating a New Record via ActiveRecord

Now we will create a new user in this table. Have a look at the following code:

```
<?
include("adodb/adodb.inc.php");
include('adodb/adodb-active-record.inc.php');
$conn =ADONewConnection('mysql');
$conn->connect("localhost","user","password","test") ;

ADODB_Active_Record::setDatabaseAdapter($conn);
class User extends ADODB_Active_Record {}
$user = new User();//a dynamic model to access the user table
$user->name = "Packt";
$user->pass = "Hello";
$user->save();//calling save() will internally save this
        //record in table
?>
```

ActiveRecord exposes a separate object for every table in your database by which you can perform different operations. Let's take a look at how we can select some data.

Selecting and Updating Data

We can load and change any record using ActiveRecord easily. Let's have a look at the following example:

```
<?
include("adodb/adodb.inc.php");
include('adodb/adodb-active-record.inc.php');
$conn =ADONewConnection('mysql');
$conn->connect("localhost","user","password","test") ;

ADODB_Active_Record::setDatabaseAdapter($conn);
class User extends ADODB_Active_Record {}
$user = new User();
$user->load("id=10");//load the record where the id is 10
echo $user->name;
$user->name= "Afif Mohiuddin";//now update
$user->save();//and save the previously loaded record
?>
```

So that's fairly easy. When you call the load() method with any expression, the record will be loaded into the object itself. Then you can make any change and finally save it. ActiveRecord is extremely charming to work with.

Summary

You finished reading a chapter devoted for total DB access using the OOP way. There are lot other interesting projects like Propel (`http://propel.phpdb.org/trac/`) as Object Relational Mapping library for PHP developers, Creole (`http://creole.phpdb.org/trac/`) as a DAL, ActiveRecord library from CodeIgniter framework (`http://www.codeigniter.com`), and many more. You have got a large number of resources available to manipulate database using PHP5 and OO style.

In the next chapter we will learn about using XML in PHP. You will be surprised to find that you can use plain XML files as a lightweight alternative of regular heavyweight database engines. Until then, happy coding.

8
Cooking XML with OOP

XML (Extensible Markup Language) is a very important format for storing multi-purpose data. It is also known as universal data format, as you can represent anything and visualize the data properly with the help of a renderer. One of the biggest advantages of XML is that it can be converted from one form of data into another easily with the help of XSLT. Also, XML data is highly readable.

One of the great blessings of PHP5 is its excellent support to manipulate XML. PHP5 comes bundled with new XML extensions for processing XML easily. You have a whole new **SimpleXML** API to read XML documents in a pure object-oriented way. Also, you have the **DOMDocument** object to parse and create XML documents. In this chapter we will learn these APIs and learn how to successfully process XML with PHP.

Formation of XML

Let us look at the structure of a common XML document in case you are totally new to XML. If you are already familiar with XML, which we greatly recommend for this chapter, then it is not a section for you.

Let's look at the following example, which represents a set of emails:

```
<?xml version="1.0" encoding="ISO-8859-1" ?>
<emails>
  <email>
    <from>nowhere@notadomain.tld</from>
    <to>unknown@unknown.tld</to>
    <subject>there is no subject</subject>
    <body>is it a body? oh ya</body>
  </email>
</emails>
```

So you see that XML documents do have a small declaration at the top which details the character set of the document. This is useful if you are storing Unicode texts. In XML, you must close the tags as you start it. (XML is strict than HTML, you must follow the conventions.)

Let's look at another example where there are some special symbols in the data:

```
<?xml version="1.0" encoding="ISO-8859-1" ?>
<emails>
  <email>
    <from>nowhere@notadomain.tld</from>
    <to>unknown@unknown.tld</to>
    <subject>there is no subject</subject>
    <body><![CDATA[is it a body? oh ya, with some texts
                                 & symbols]]></body>
  </email>
</emails>
```

This means you have to enclose all the strings containing special characters with CDATA.

Again, each entity may have some attributes with it. For example consider the following XML where we describe the properties of a student:

```
<student age= "17" class= "11" title= "Mr.">Ozniak</student>
```

In the above example, there are three attributes to this student tag—age, class, and title. Using PHP we can easily manipulate them too. In the coming sections we will learn how to parse XML documents, or how to create XML documents on the fly.

Introduction to SimpleXML

In PHP4 there were two ways to parse XML documents, and these are also available in PHP5. One is parsing documents via SAX (which is a standard) and another one is DOM. But it takes quite a long time to parse XML documents using SAX and it also needs quite a long time for you to write the code.

In PHP5 a new API has been introduced to easily parse XML documents. This was named SimpleXML API. Using SimpleXML API you can turn your XML documents into an array. Each node will be converted to an accessible form for easy parsing.

Parsing Documents

In this section we will learn how to parse basic XML documents using SimpleXML. Let's take a breath and start.

```
<?
$str = <<< END
<emails>
  <email>
    <from>nowhere@notadomain.tld</from>
    <to>unknown@unknown.tld</to>
    <subject>there is no subject</subject>
    <body><![CDATA[is it a body? oh ya, with some texts &
                                    symbols]]></body>
  </email>
</emails>
END;
$sxml = simplexml_load_string($str);
print_r($sxml);
?>
```

The output is like this:

```
SimpleXMLElement Object
(
    [email] => SimpleXMLElement Object
        (
            [from] => nowhere@notadomain.tld
            [to] => unknown@unknown.tld
            [subject] => there is no subject
            [body] => SimpleXMLElement Object
                (
                )

        )

)
```

So now you can ask how to access each of these properties individually. You can access each of them like an object. For example, $sxml->email[0] returns the first email object. To access the from element under this email, you can use the following code like:

```
echo $sxml->email[0]->from
```

So, each object, unless available more than once, can be accessed just by its name. Otherwise you have to access them like a collection. For example, if you have multiple elements, you can access each of them using a `foreach` loop:

```
foreach ($sxml->email as $email)
echo $email->from;
```

Accessing Attributes

As we saw in the previous example, XML nodes may have attributes. Remember the example document with `class`, `age`, and `title`? Now you can easily access these attributes using SimpleXML API. Let's see the following example:

```
<?
$str = <<< END
<emails>
  <email type="mime">
    <from>nowhere@notadomain.tld</from>
    <to>unknown@unknown.tld</to>
    <subject>there is no subject</subject>
    <body><![CDATA[is it a body? oh ya, with some texts &
                                    symbols]]></body>
  </email>
</emails>
END;
$sxml = simplexml_load_string($str);
foreach ($sxml->email as $email)
echo $email['type'];
?>
```

This will display the text `mime` in the output window. So if you look carefully, you will understand that each node is accessible like properties of an object, and all attributes are accessed like keys of an array. SimpleXML makes XML parsing really fun.

Parsing Flickr Feeds using SimpleXML

How about adding some milk and sugar to your coffee? So far we have learned what SimpleXML API is and how to make use of it. It would be much better if we could see a practical example. In this example we will parse the Flickr feeds and display the pictures. Sounds cool? Let's do it.

If you are interested what the Flickr public photo feed looks like, here is the content. The feed data is collected from `http://www.flickr.com/services/feeds/photos_public.gne`:

```
<?xml version="1.0" encoding="utf-8" standalone="yes"?>
<feed xmlns="http://www.w3.org/2005/Atom"
      xmlns:dc="http://purl.org/dc/elements/1.1/" >
  <title>Everyone's photos</title>
  <link rel="self"
   href="http://www.flickr.com/services/feeds/photos_public.gne" />
  <link rel="alternate" type="text/html"
     href="http://www.flickr.com/photos/"/>
  <id>tag:flickr.com,2005:/photos/public</id>
  <icon>http://www.flickr.com/images/buddyicon.jpg</icon>
  <subtitle></subtitle>
  <updated>2007-07-18T12:44:52Z</updated>
  <generator uri="http://www.flickr.com/">Flickr</generator>
  <entry>
    <title>A-lounge 9.07_6</title>
    <link rel="alternate" type="text/html"
       href="http://www.flickr.com/photos/dimitranova/845455130/"/>
    <id>tag:flickr.com,2005:/photo/845455130</id>
    <published>2007-07-18T12:44:52Z</published>
    <updated>2007-07-18T12:44:52Z</updated>
          <dc:date.Taken>2007-07-09T14:22:55-08:00</dc:date.Taken>
    <content type="html">&lt;p&gt;&lt;a
    href=&quot;http://www.flickr.com/people/dimitranova/&quot;
    &gt;Dimitranova&lt;/a&gt; posted a photo:&lt;/p&gt;
    &lt;p&gt;&lt;a
       href=&quot;http://www.flickr.com/photos/dimitranova/845455130/
    &quot; title=&quot;A-lounge 9.07_6&quot;&gt;&lt;img src=&quot;
    http://farm2.static.flickr.com/1285/845455130_dce61d101f_m.jpg
    &quot; width=&quot;180&quot; height=&quot;240&quot; alt=&quot;
    A-lounge 9.07_6&quot; /&gt;&lt;/a&gt;&lt;/p&gt;
</content>
        <author>
          <name>Dimitranova</name>
          <uri>http://www.flickr.com/people/dimitranova/</uri>
        </author>
        <link rel="license" type="text/html" href="deed.en-us" />
          <link rel="enclosure" type="image/jpeg"
           href="http://farm2.static.flickr.com/1285/
                                845455130_7ef3a3415d_o.jpg" />
  </entry>
  <entry>
    <title>DSC00375</title>
    <link rel="alternate" type="text/html"
     href="http://www.flickr.com/photos/53395103@N00/845454986/"/>
    <id>tag:flickr.com,2005:/photo/845454986</id>
    <published>2007-07-18T12:44:50Z</published>
    ...
  </entry>
</feed>
```

Now we will extract the description from each entry and display it. Let's have some fun:

```
<?
$content =
  file_get_contents(
    "http://www.flickr.com/services/feeds/photos_public.gne ");
$sx = simplexml_load_string($content);
foreach ($sx->entry as $entry)
{
  echo "<a href='{$entry->link['href']}'>".$entry->title."</a><br/>";
  echo $entry->content."<br/>";
}
?>
```

This will create the following output. See, how easy SimpleXML is? The output of the above script is shown below:

Managing CDATA Sections using SimpleXML

As we said before, some symbols can't appear directly as a value of any node unless you enclose them using CDATA tag. For example, take a look at following example:

```
<?
$str = <<<EOT
<data>
  <content>text & images </content>
</data>
EOT;
$s = simplexml_load_string($str);
?>
```

This will generate the following error:

```
<br />
<b>Warning</b>:  simplexml_load_string()
    [<a href='function.simplexml-load-string'>
      function.simplexml-load-string</a>]:
    Entity: line 2: parser error : xmlParseEntityRef:
    no name in <b>C:\OOP with PHP5\Codes\ch8\cdata.php</b>
    on line <b>10</b><br /><br />
<b>Warning</b>:  simplexml_load_string()
    [<a href='function.simplexml-load-string'>
      function.simplexml-load-string</a>]:
    &lt;content&gt;text &amp; images &lt;/content&gt;
    in <b>C:\OOP with PHP5\Codes\ch8\cdata.php</b>
    on line <b>10</b><br /><br />
<b>Warning</b>:  simplexml_load_string()
    [<a href='function.simplexml-load-string'>
      function.simplexml-load-string</a>]:
    ^ in <b>C:\OOP with PHP5\Codes\ch8\cdata.php</b>
    on line <b>10</b><br />
```

To avoid this problem we have to enclose using a CDATA tag. Let's rewrite it like this:

```
<data>
  <content><![CDATA[text & images ]]></content>
</data>
```

Now it will work perfectly. And you don't have to do any extra work for managing this CDATA section.

```
<?
$str = <<<EOT
<data>
  <content><![CDATA[text & images ]]></content>
</data>
EOT;
$s = simplexml_load_string($str);
echo $s->content;//print "text & images"
?>
```

However, prior to PHP5.1, you had to load this section as shown below:

```
$s = simplexml_load_string($str,null,LIBXML_NOCDATA);
```

XPath

Another nice addition in SimpleXML is that you can query using XPath. So what is XPath? It's an expression language that helps you to locate specific nodes using formatted input. In this section we will learn how to locate a specific part of our XML documents using SimpleXML and Xpath. Let's have a look at the following XML:

```
<?xml version="1.0" encoding="utf-8"?>
<roles>
  <task type="analysis">
    <state name="new">
      <assigned to="cto">
        <action newstate="clarify" assignedto="pm">
          <notify>pm</notify>
          <notify>cto</notify>
        </action>
      </assigned>
    </state>
    <state name="clarify">
      <assigned to="pm">
        <action newstate="clarified" assignedto="pm">
          <notify>cto</notify>
        </action>
      </assigned>
    </state>
  </task>
</roles>
```

This document simply states the workflow of an analysis task and then tells it what to do at which state. So now you want to search what to do when the task type is `analysis` and assigned to `cto` and current state is `new`. SimpleXML makes it really easy. Let's take a look at the following code:

```
<?
$str = <<< EOT
<roles>
  <task type="analysis">
    <state name="new">
      <assigned to="cto">
        <action newstate="clarify" assignedto="pm">
          <notify>pm</notify>
          <notify>cto</notify>
        </action>
      </assigned>
    </state>
    <state name="clarify">
      <assigned to="pm">
        <action newstate="clarified" assignedto="pm">
          <notify>cto</notify>
        </action>
      </assigned>
    </state>
  </task>
</roles>
EOT;

$s = simplexml_load_string($str);
$node = $s->xpath("//task[@type='analysis']/state[@name='new']
                                      /assigned[@to='cto']");
echo $node[0]->action[0]['newstate']."\n";
echo $node[0]->action[0]->notify[0];
?>
```

This will echo the following:

```
clarify
pm
```

However there is something to remember while writing XPath. When your XPath is followed by / then it means that you should keep the exact sequence of your XML document. For example:

```
echo count($s->xpath("//state"));
```

This will output 2.

`//state` means take the state node from anywhere in the document. Now if you specify `task//state`, it will return all states from under all tasks. For example the following code will output 3 and 3:

```
echo count($s->xpath("//notify"));
echo count($s->xpath("task//notify"));
```

Now what if you want to find `notify` just under `state`, following `assigned`, following `action`? Your XPath query should be `//state/assigned/action/notify`.

But if you want that, it should be exactly under the `task` node which is just under the root node, it should be `/task/state/assigned/action/notify`.

If you need to match any attribute then match it as `[@AttributeName1='value'] [@AttributeName2='value']`. If you see the following XPath, it will be clear to you:

```
//task[@type='analysis']/state[@name='new']/assigned[@to='cto']
```

DOM API

SimpleXML in PHP is used to parse the document however it cannot create any XML document. For creating XML documents on the fly you have to use DOM API that comes bundled with PHP 5. Using DOM API you can also create page-scrapping tools fairly easily.

In this section we will learn how to create XML documents using DOM API, and then we will learn how to parse existing documents and modify them.

In the following example we will create just a basic HTML file:

```
<?
    $doc = new DOMDocument("1.0","UTF-8");
    $html = $doc->createElement("html");
    $body = $doc->createElement("body");
    $h1 = $doc->createElement("h1","OOP with PHP");
    $body->appendChild($h1);
    $html->appendChild($body);
    $doc->appendChild($html);
    echo $doc->saveHTML();
?>
```

This will produce the following code:

```
<html>
  <body>
    <h1>OOP with PHP</h1>
  </body>
</html>
```

That's fairly easy, right?

Let's do some more:

```
<?
    $doc = new DOMDocument("1.0","UTF-8");
    $html = $doc->createElement("html");
    $body = $doc->createElement("body");
    $h1 = $doc->createElement("h1","OOP with PHP");
    $h1->setAttribute("id","firsth1");
    $p = $doc->createElement("p");
    $p->appendChild($doc->createTextNode("Hi - how about some text?"));
    $body->appendChild($h1);
    $body->appendChild($p);
    $html->appendChild($body);
    $doc->appendChild($html);
    echo $doc->saveHTML();
?>
```

This will produce the following code.

```
<html><body>
  <h1 id="firsth1">OOP with PHP</h1>
  <p>Hi - how about some text?</p>
</body></html>
```

So you can save this XML generated by the DOM engine using the following code entered into a file in your file system:

```
file_put_contents("c:/abc.xml", $doc->saveHTML());
```

Modifying Existing Documents

DOM API helps to create XML document easily as well as provide easy access to load and modify existing documents. With the following XML we will load the file we just created a few minutes ago and then we will change the header test of the first `h1` object:

```php
<?php
$uri = 'c:/abc.xml';
$document = new DOMDocument();
$document->loadHTMLFile($uri);// load the content of this URL as HTML
$h1s = $document->getElementsByTagName("h1");//find all h1 elements
$newText = $document->createElement("h1","New Heading");//created a
                                                   //new h1 element
$h1s->item(0)->parentNode->insertBefore($newText,
$h1s->item(0));//insert before the existing h1 element
$h1s->item(0)->parentNode->removeChild($h1s->item(1));//remove the
                                                   //old h1 element
echo $document->saveHTML();//display the content as HTML
?>
```

The output is shown below:

```
<!DOCTYPE html PUBLIC "-//W3C//DTD HTML 4.0 Transitional//EN"
"http://www.w3.org/TR/REC-html40/loose.dtd">
<html><body>
<h1>New Heading</h1>
<p>Hi - how about some text?</p>
</body></html>
```

Other Useful Functions

There are some other useful functions in the DOM library. We are not going to discuss them in depth, however they are included in this section for a one line overview.

- `DomNode->setAttribute()`: Helps to set the attribute of any node

- `DomNode->hasChildNodes()`: Returns true if a DOM node has a child node

- `DomNode->replaceChild()`: Replaces any child node with another one

- `DomNode->cloneNode()`: Creates a deep copy of the current code

Summary

XML API in PHP5 plays a very important role in web application development, most notably the new SimpleXML API, which simplifies parsing with ease. Today XML is one of the most used data formats for almost all big applications. Therefore getting familiar with XML APIs and relevant technologies will definitely help you to design robust XML-based applications more easily.

In the next chapter we will learn about MVC architecture and build a slick MVC framework on our own.

9
Building Better with MVC

In chapter 4 we learned how design patterns can simplify your daily programming life by providing you with common approaches for solving problems. One of the popular design patterns used for application architecture is **Model-View-Controller,** which is also known as **MVC**. In RAD (Rapid Application Development) for PHP, MVC frameworks play a vital role. These days several MVC frameworks have gained public interest and many of them are enterprise-ready. For example, **symfony** framework has been used in developing Yahoo bookmarks, CakePHP is being developed in refactoring Mambo, CodeIgniter is used by many big applications showcased on their site. Also there are popular MVC frameworks like Zend Framework, which is used by IBM and also used to develop the Magento open-source ecommerce solution.

Therefore, nowadays, writing code from scratch and fine tuning it is obsolete, and if you are doing this, you should really avoid it. In this chapter, we will discuss the basic structure of MVC frameworks and then introduce you to some of these popular frameworks.

What is MVC?

As the name implies, MVC consists of three components. The first one is Model, the second one is View, and the third one is Controller. This doesn't make any sense if we just list the names. To begin with, Model is an object, which interacts with a database. All business logics are usually written inside the model. A controller is a piece of code, which takes user inputs and based on that initializes models and other objects, and finally invokes all of them. Finally, the View is a component, which displays the result generated by controller with the help of model.

So for good practice, you should never implement any business logic in view or controller. Similarly, you should never process the output results in a model. And you should never produce any output directly from controller (instead use the view).

In the following sections we will be creating a very small MVC.

Planning for the Project

For successfully developing any application you must have a clear target. Whenever the architecture of an application is robust, stable, and foolproof, you will get a huge number of users using your application. The MVC framework we are going to develop in this chapter will serve the following issues successfully:

- Small footprint
- Easy loading of components, libraries, helpers, and models
- Nice and flexible syntax for developing view
- Excellent support with popular database servers
- Will not be resource extensive
- Easy to use
- Easy to integrate with other component frameworks like Pear, ezComponents, and so on.
- Support for caching
- Layout support like RubyOnRails for easy design of your web application
- A native gzip compressor for JavaScript
- Ajax support

Designing the Bootstrap File

The bootstrap is a file, which just prepares the environment for successful execution and integration of controllers, models, and views. Basically a bootstrap file initializes the environment, the router, the object loader, and passes all the input parameters to the controller. We will design the bootstrap file, which will receive all the parameters of a successful request URL with the help of mod_rewrite.

 mod_rewrite is an apache module, which helps to redirect a request defined by a pattern (regular expression) to another request URL. It is an essential module for almost every web application designed. If you are interested in studying more on it, you can go to: http://httpd.apache.org/docs/2.0/mod/mod_rewrite.html

To enable `mod_rewrite` you can follow the following details. Firstly, open `httpd.conf` and add the following lines:

```
LoadModule rewrite_module modules/mod_rewrite.so
<Directory />
    Options FollowSymLinks
    AllowOverride None
    Order deny,allow
    Deny from all
    Satisfy all
</Directory>
```

We have to place the following code in an `.htaccess` file and place it inside our application root.

```
RewriteEngine on
RewriteCond $1 !^(index\.php|images|robots\.txt)
RewriteCond %{REQUEST_FILENAME} !-f
RewriteCond %{REQUEST_FILENAME} !-d
RewriteRule ^(.*)$ index.php?$1
```

This code will just redirect every request to `index.php`, which will be our bootstrap file. This bootstrap file will receive any requested URL and then split it into different parts like controller, action and parameters. For example, the format will be `http://our_application/controller/action/param/param..../param`. The bootstrap will analyze the URL with the help of a router and then with the help of dispatcher it will invoke controller and action with all the parameters.

Here is the code of our bootstrap file (`index.php`):

```
<?
include("core/ini.php");
initializer::initialize();
$router = loader::load("router");
dispatcher::dispatch($router);
?>
```

In the above code you see that there is an object called `loader`. The main purpose of this is to load objects for us, but via the Singleton pattern. This will help us to minimize the load. Using this loader we will load an object named `router`. There is also an object called `dispatcher`, which will finally dispatch the web request with the help of router.

Let's check the code of `core/ini.php`, which is a helper to help easy inclusion of class files from different directories.

```
<?
set_include_path(get_include_path().PATH_SEPARATOR."core/main");
function __autoload($object)
{
  require_once("{$object}.php");
}
?>
```

Here goes the `initializer` file (`core/main/initializer.php`):

```
<?
class initializer
{
  public static function initialize()
  {
  set_include_path(get_include_path().PATH_SEPARATOR."core/main");
  set_include_path(get_include_path().PATH_SEPARATOR.
                                      "core/main/cache");
  set_include_path(get_include_path().PATH_SEPARATOR."core/helpers");
  set_include_path(get_include_path().PATH_SEPARATOR.
                                      "core/libraries");
  //set_include_path(get_include_path().PATH_SEPARATOR.
                                      "app/controllers");
  set_include_path(get_include_path().PATH_SEPARATOR."app/models");
  set_include_path(get_include_path().PATH_SEPARATOR."app/views");
//include_once("core/config/config.php");
  }
}
?>
```

If you take a look at the code of the `initializer` file, you will find that it actually just extends the include path.

Here is the code of our `loader` file (`core/main/loader.php`), which will load different components via the Singleton pattern.

```
<?
class loader
{
  private static $loaded = array();
  public static function load($object)
  {
    $valid = array(    "library",
```

```
        "view",
        "model",
        "helper",
        "router",
        "config",
        "hook",
        "cache",
        "db");
        if (!in_array($object,$valid))
        {
          $config = self::load("config");
          if ("on"==$config->debug)
          {
            base::backtrace();
          }
  throw new Exception("Not a valid object '{$object}' to load");
        }
        if (empty(self::$loaded[$object])){
          self::$loaded[$object]= new $object();
        }
        return self::$loaded[$object];
    }
}
?>
```

Loader uses another `config` file (`core/main/config.php`), which actually loads different `configs` from under `config/configs.php` file:

```
<?
class config
{
  private $config;
  function __construct()
  {
    global $configs;
    include_once("core/config/configs.php");
    include_once("app/config/configs.php");
    $this->config = $configs;
  }
  private function __get($var)
  {
    return $this->config[$var];
  }
}
?>
```

If you wonder how our `configs.php` will look, here it goes:

```
<?
$configs['debug']="on";
$configs['base_url']="http://localhost/orchid";
$configs['global_profile']=true;
$configs['allowed_url_chars'] = "/[^A-z0-9\/\^]/";
$configs['default_controller']="welcome";
?>
```

Well, if you look at the code of `loader.php` there is a section like this:

```
$config = self::load("config");
  if ("on"==$config->debug)
    {
      base::backtrace();
    }
```

So `$config->debug` actually returns the value of `$configs['debug']` with the help of `__get()` magic method in `config.php`.

In loader there is a method named `base::backtrace()`. `base` is a static object declared in `core/libraries/base.php`. It contains some useful functions to use throughout the framework. This is in `core/libraries/base.php`:

```
<?
class base{
  public static function pr($array)
  {
    echo "<pre>";
    print_r($array);
    echo "</pre>";
  }
  public static function backtrace()
  {
    echo "<pre>";
    debug_print_backtrace();
    echo "</pre>";
  }
  public static function basePath()
  {
    return getcwd();
  }
  public static function baseUrl()
  {
    $conf = loader::load("config");
    return $conf->base_url;
  }
?>
```

Therefore `base::backtrace()` actually prints `debug_backtrace` for easy tracing exceptions.

So far we haven't seen the code of `router.php` and `dispatcher.php`. Router and dispatcher are the main part of the whole application. Here is the code of `router.php` (`core/main/router.php`):

```php
<?
class router
{
  private $route;
  private $controller;
  private $action;
  private $params;
  public function __construct()
  {
    if(file_exists("app/config/routes.php")){
      require_once("app/config/routes.php");
    }
    $path = array_keys($_GET);
    $config = loader::load("config");
    if (!isset($path[0]))
    {
      $default_controller = $config->default_controller;
      if (!empty($default_controller))
      $path[0] = $default_controller;
      else
      $path[0] = "index";
    }
    $route= $path[0];
    $sanitzing_pattern = $config->allowed_url_chars;
    $route = preg_replace($sanitzing_pattern, "", $route);
    $route = str_replace("^","",$route);
    $this->route = $route;
    $routeParts = split( "/",$route);
    $this->controller=$routeParts[0];
    $this->action=isset($routeParts[1])? $routeParts[1]:"base";
    array_shift($routeParts);
    array_shift($routeParts);
    $this->params=$routeParts;
    /* match user defined routing pattern */
    if (isset($routes)){
      foreach ($routes as $_route)
      {
        $_pattern = "~{$_route[0]}~";
```

```
            $_destination = $_route[1];
            if (preg_match($_pattern,$route))
            {
              $newrouteparts = split("/",$_destination);
              $this->controller = $newrouteparts[0];
              $this->action = $newrouteparts[1];
            }
          }
        }
      }
    }
    public function getAction()
    {
      if (empty($this->action)) $this->action="main";
      return $this->action;
    }
    public function getController()
    {
      return $this->controller;
    }
    public function getParams()
    {
      return $this->params;
    }
  }
?>
```

What router actually does is find the controller, action, and parameters from a request URL. If the controller name is not found, it uses the default controller name and if default controller name is not found in config file, it will use index as the default controller.

Before proceeding to dispatcher, we must look at the view engine, which will be used for template engine, so that anyone from controller can set variables like this $this->view->set(varname, value). After that, anyone can access the variable as $varname in our view file.

So here comes the view engine (core/main/view.php):

```
<?
class view
{
  private $vars=array();
  private $template;
  public function set($key, $value)
```

```
  {
  $this->vars[$key]=$value;
  }
  public function getVars(&$controller=null)
  {
    if (!empty($controller)) $this->vars['app']=$controller;
    return $this->vars;
  }
  public function setTemplate($template)
  {
    $this->template = $template;
  }
  public function getTemplate($controller=null)
  {
    if (empty($this->template)) return $controller;
    return $this->template;
  }
  private function __get($var)
  {
    return loader::load($var);
  }
  }
  ?>
```

Here comes the dispatcher, the core part of our framework
(core/main/dispatcher.php):

```
  <?
  class dispatcher
  {
    public static function dispatch($router)
    {
      global $app;
      //$cache = loader::load("cache");
      ob_start();
      $config = loader::load("config");
      if ($config->global_profile) $start = microtime(true);
      $controller = $router->getController();
      $action = $router->getAction();
      $params = $router->getParams();
      if (count($params)>1){
        if ("unittest"==$params[count($params)-1] ||
                   '1'==$_POST['unittest'])unittest::setUp();
```

```
    }
    $controllerfile = "app/controllers/{$controller}.php";
    if (file_exists($controllerfile)){
        require_once($controllerfile);
        $app = new $controller();

        $app->use_layout = true;

        $app->setParams($params);

        $app->$action();

        unittest::tearDown();

        ob_end_clean();

        //manage view
        ob_start();
        $view = loader::load("view");
        $viewvars = $view->getVars($app);
        $uselayout = $config->use_layout;

        if (!$app->use_layout) $uselayout=false;

        $template = $view->getTemplate($action);
        base::_loadTemplate($controller, $template,
                                $viewvars, $uselayout);

        if (isset($start))
    echo "<p>Total time for dispatching is :
            ".(microtime(true)-$start)." seconds.</p>";
        $output = ob_get_clean();

        //$cache->set("abcde",array
                    ("content"=>base64_encode($output)));
        echo $output;
    }
    else
    throw new Exception("Controller not found");
    }
}
?>
```

Here's what dispatcher mainly does (as seen from the highlighted section of the above code). It takes a router object as parameter then finds controller, action, and parameters from router. If the controller file is available, it loads that and then initializes the controller. After initializing, it just accesses the action.

After that, dispatcher initializes the current view object using loader. As it is coming via Singleton, all variables set to it are still in scope. Dispatcher then passes the view template file, variables to a function named `_loadTemplate` in base.

So what is the purpose of `$uselayout`? It just indicates whether a layout file should be appended to our template. This is more fun when we see it in practice.

Here is the `base::_loadTemplate()` function:

```
public static function _loadTemplate($controller, $template,
                                     $vars, $uselayout=false)
{
  extract($vars);
  if ($uselayout)
  ob_start();
  $templatefile ="app/views/{$controller}/{$template}.php";
  if (file_exists($templatefile)){
    include_once($templatefile);
  }
  else
  {
    throw new Exception("View '{$template}.php' is not found in
                         views/{$controller} directory.");
  }
  if ($uselayout) {
    $layoutdata = ob_get_clean();
    $layoutfilelocal = "app/views/{$controller}/{$controller}.php";
    $layoutfileglobal = "app/views/layouts/{$controller}.php";

    if (file_exists($layoutfilelocal))
    include_once($layoutfilelocal);
    else
    include_once($layoutfileglobal);
  }
}
```

If you are confused about placing these files, here is the directory structure to help you understand:

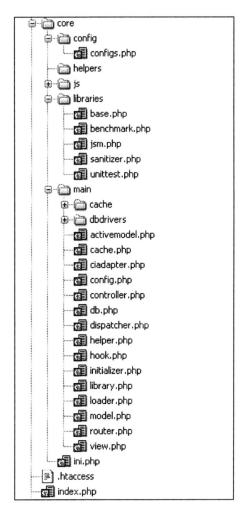

Why are there other files like jsm.php, benchmark.php, unittest.php, helper.php, model.php, library.php, cache.php, and db.php?

- These files will help us for the following sections:
- jsm.php: Helps to load JavaScript with automatic gzip compression
- db.php: For connecting to different database
- library.php: Helps to load library files
- unittest.php: Will help to automate unit testing
- model.php: Will help to load models for database access

Now let's see what our model and library are doing.

Here comes core/main/model.php:

```php
<?
class model
{
  private $loaded = array();
  private function __get($model)
  {
    $model .="model";
    $modelfile = "app/models/{$model}.php";
    $config = loader::load("config");
    if (file_exists($modelfile))
    {
      include_once($modelfile);
      if (empty($this->loaded[$model]))
      {
        $this->loaded[$model]=new $model();
      }
      $modelobj = $this->loaded[$model];
      if ($config->auto_model_association)
      {
        $this->associate($modelobj, $_REQUEST); //auto association
      }
      return $modelobj;
    }
    else
    {
      throw new Exception("Model {$model} is not found");
    }
  }
  private function associate(&$obj, $array)
  {
    foreach ($array as $key=>$value)
    {
      if (property_exists($obj, $key))
      {
        $obj->$key = $value;
      }
    }
  }
}
?>
```

Whenever a form is submitted, we want to populate any model right after initializing it. Therefore, we have kept a configuration variable named auto_model_ association for it. If you set it to true, models will be automatically associated.

Here comes the library loader (core/main/library.php):

```
<?
class library{
  private $loaded = array();
  private function __get($lib)
  {
    if (empty($this->loaded[$lib]))
    {
      $libnamecore = "core/libraries/{$lib}.php";
      $libnameapp = "app/libraries/{$lib}.php";
      if (file_exists($libnamecore))
      {
        require_once($libnamecore);
        $this->loaded[$lib]=new $lib();
      }
      else if(file_exists($libnameapp))
      {
        require_once($libnameapp);
        $this->loaded[$lib]=new $lib();
      }
      else
      {
        throw new Exception("Library {$lib} not found.");
      }
    }
    return $this->loaded[$lib];
  }
}
?>
```

library.php helps only to load libraries via a Singleton.

Now we will see the JavaScript loader, which by default delivers each library with gzip compression. These days every browser supports gzip compression for faster loading of any object. We are also distributing distributing our framework with built-in support for prototype, jQuery and script.aculo.us.

Here is `core/libraries/jsm.php`:

```php
<?
/**
 * Javascript Manager
 *
 */
class jsm
{
  function loadPrototype()
  {
    $base = base::baseUrl();
    echo "<script type='text/javascript'
          src='{$base}/core/js/gzip.php?js=prototypec.js'>\n";
  }
  function loadScriptaculous()
  {
    $base = base::baseUrl();
    echo "<script type='text/javascript'
      src='{$base}/core/js/gzip.php?js=scriptaculousc.js'>\n";
  }
  function loadProtaculous()
  {
    $base = base::baseUrl();
    echo "<script type='text/javascript'
      src='{$base}/core/js/gzip.php?js=prototypec.js'>\n";
    echo "<script type='text/javascript'
      src='{$base}/core/js/gzip.php?js=scriptaculousc.js'>\n";
  }
  function loadJquery()
  {
    $base = base::baseUrl();
    echo "<script type='text/javascript'
          src='{$base}/core/js/gzip.php?js=jqueryc.js'>\n";
  }
  /**
   * app specific libraries
   *
   * @param string $filename
   */
  function loadScript($filename)
  {
    $base = base::baseUrl();
    $script = $base."/app/js/{$filename}.js";
    echo "<script type='text/javascript'
          src='{$base}/core/js/gzip.php?js={$script}'>\n";
  }
}
?>
```

If you take a look at the code you will find that it loads every JavaScript file via gzip.php, which is actually responsible for compressing the content. So here is the code of gzip.php (core/js/gzip.php):

```php
<?php
ob_start("ob_gzhandler");
header("Content-type: text/javascript; charset: UTF-8");
header("Cache-Control: must-revalidate");
$offset = 60 * 60 * 24 * 3;
$ExpStr = "Expires: " .
        gmdate("D, d M Y H:i:s",  time() + $offset) . " GMT";
header($ExpStr);
$js = $_GET['js'];
if (in_array($js,
     array("prototypec.js","scriptaculousc.js","jqueryc.js")))
                         include(urldecode($_GET['js']));
?>
```

If you have other libraries to load, you can modify this library and add them in the following line.

```php
if (in_array($js,
   array("prototypec.js","scriptaculousc.js","jqueryc.js")))
```

Lastly, we have another file, which helps us writing a unit test during the developing of our application. unittest.php is responsible for that and there is also a Boolean configuration flag for this: unit_test_enabled.

Here is core/main/unittest.php:

```php
<?
class unittest
{
  private static $results = array();
  private static $testmode = false;
  public static function setUp()
  {
    $config = loader::load("config");
    if ($config->unit_test_enabled){
      self::$results = array();
      self::$testmode = true;
    }
  }
  public static function tearDown()
  {
```

```php
    if (self::$testmode)
    {
      self::printTestResult();
      self::$results = array();
      self::$testmode = false;
      die();
    }
  }
  public static function printTestResult()
  {
    foreach (self::$results as $result)
    {
      echo $result."<hr/>";
    }
  }
  public static function assertTrue($object)
  {
    if (!self::$testmode) return 0;
    if (true==$object) $result = "passed";
    self::saveResult(true, $object, $result);
  }
  public static function assertEqual($object, $constant)
  {
    if (!self::$testmode) return 0;
    if ($object==$constant)
    {
      $result = 1;
    }
    self::saveResult($constant, $object, $result);
  }
  private static function getTrace()
  {
    $result = debug_backtrace();
    $cnt = count($result);
    $callerfile = $result[2]['file'];
    $callermethod = $result[3]['function'];
    $callerline = $result[2]['line'];
    return array($callermethod, $callerline, $callerfile);
  }
  private static function saveResult($expected, $actual,
                                                  $result=false)
  {
    if (empty($actual)) $actual = "null/false";
    if ("failed"==$result || empty($result))
```

```php
    $result = "<font color='red'><strong>failed</strong></font>";
    else
    $result = "<font color='green'><strong>passed</strong></font>";
    $trace = self::getTrace();
    $finalresult = "Test {$result} in Method:
        <strong>{$trace[0]}</strong>. Line:
        <strong>{$trace[1]}</strong>. File:
        <strong>{$trace[2]}</strong>. <br/> Expected:
        <strong>{$expected}</strong>, Actual:
        <strong>{$actual}</strong>. ";
    self::$results[] = $finalresult;
}
public static function assertArrayHasKey($key, array $array,
                                                        $message = '')
{
    if (!self::$testmode) return 0;
    if (array_key_exists($key, $array))
    {
        $result = 1;
        self::saveResult("Array has a key named '{$key}'",
                    "Array has a key named '{$key}'", $result);
        return ;
    }
    self::saveResult("Array has a key named '{$key}'",
                "Array has not a key named '{$key}'", $result);
}
public static function assertArrayNotHasKey($key, array $array,
                                                        $message = '')
{
    if (!self::$testmode) return 0;
    if (!array_key_exists($key, $array))
    {
        $result = 1;
        self::saveResult("Array has not a key named '{$key}'",
                "Array has not a key named '{$key}'", $result);
        return ;
    }
    self::saveResult("Array has not a key named '{$key}'",
                    "Array has a key named '{$key}'", $result);
}
public static function assertContains($needle, $haystack,
                            $message = '')
{
```

```
        if (!self::$testmode) return 0;
        if (in_array($needle,$haystack))
        {
          $result = 1;
          self::saveResult("Array has a needle named '{$needle}'",
                  "Array has a needle named '{$needle}'", $result);
          return ;
        }
        self::saveResult("Array has a needle named '{$needle}'",
                "Array has not a needle named '{$needle}'", $result);
    }
  }
?>
```

We must keep a built-in support for benchmarking our code to help profiling.
Therefore, we have benchmark.php (core/main/benchmark.php) which performs it:

```
<?
class benchmark
{
  private $times = array();
  private $keys = array();
  public function setMarker($key=null)
  {
    $this->keys[] = $key;
    $this->times[] = microtime(true);
  }
  public function initiate()
  {
    $this->keys= array();
    $this->times= array();
  }
  public function printReport()
  {
    $cnt = count($this->times);
    $result = "";
    for ($i=1; $i<$cnt; $i++)
    {
      $key1 = $this->keys[$i-1];
      $key2 = $this->keys[$i];
      $seconds = $this->times[$i]-$this->times[$i-1];
      $result .= "For step '{$key1}' to '{$key2}' : {$seconds}
                                        seconds.</br>";
    }
```

```
            $total = $this->times[$i-1]-$this->times[0];
            $result .= "Total time  : {$total} seconds.</br>";
            echo $result;
        }
    }
?>
```

Adding Database Support

Our framework must have a data abstraction layer to facilitate database operations
painlessly. We are going to provide support to three popular databases: SQLite,
PostgreSQL, and MySQL. Here is the code of our data abstraction layer in
core/main/db.php:

```
<?
include_once("dbdrivers/abstract.dbdriver.php");
class db
{
    private $dbengine;
    private $state  = "development";
    public function __construct()
    {
        $config = loader::load("config");
        $dbengineinfo = $config->db;
        if (!$dbengineinfo['usedb']==false)
        {
            $driver = $dbengineinfo[$this->state]['dbtype'].'driver';
            include_once("dbdrivers/{$driver}.php");
            $dbengine = new $driver($dbengineinfo[$this->state]);
            $this->dbengine = $dbengine;
        }
    }
    public function setDbState($state)
    {
        //must be 'development'/'production'/'test' or whatever
        if (empty($this->dbengine)) return 0;
        $config = loader::load("config");
        $dbengineinfo = $config->db;
        if (isset($dbengineinfo[$state]))
        {
            $this->state = $state;
        }
        else
```

```
        {
          throw new Exception("No such state in config filed called
                                        ['db']['{$state}']");
        }
    }
    private function __call($method, $args)
    {
      if (empty($this->dbengine)) return 0;
      if (!method_exists($this, $method))
      return call_user_func_array(array($this->dbengine,
                                        $method),$args);
    }
    /*private function __get($property)
    {
      if (property_exists($this->dbengine,$property))
      return $this->dbengine->$property;
    }*/
}
?>
```

It uses an abstract driver object to ensure the extensibility and consistency of the driver objects. In the future, if any third-party developer wants to introduce new drivers he must extend it in core/main/dbdrivers/abstract.dbdriver.php:

```
<?
define ("FETCH_ASSOC",1);
define ("FETCH_ROW",2);
define ("FETCH_BOTH",3);
define ("FETCH_OBJECT",3);
abstract class abstractdbdriver
{
  protected $connection;
  protected $results = array();
  protected $lasthash = "";
  public function count()
  {
    return 0;
  }
  public function execute($sql)
  {
    return false;
  }
  private function prepQuery($sql)
```

```
        {
          return $sql;
        }
        public function escape($sql)
        {
          return $sql;
        }
        public function affectedRows()
        {
          return 0;
        }
        public function insertId()
        {
          return 0;
        }
        public function transBegin()
        {
          return false;
        }
        public function transCommit()
        {
        return false;
        }
        public function transRollback()
        {
          return false;
        }
        public function getRow($fetchmode = FETCH_ASSOC)
        {
          return array();
        }
        public function getRowAt($offset=null,$fetchmode = FETCH_ASSOC)
        {
          return array();
        }
        public function rewind()
        {
          return false;
        }
        public function getRows($start, $count, $fetchmode = FETCH_ASSOC)
        {
          return array();
        }
    }
    ?>
```

Drivers

Now here comes the trickiest part; the drivers. Let's take a look at SQLite driver file
`core/main/dbdrivers/sqlitedriver.php`:

```php
<?
class sqlitedriver extends abstractdbdriver
{
  public function __construct($dbinfo)
  {
    if (isset($dbinfo['dbname']))
    {
      if (!$dbinfo['persistent'])
      $this->connection =
            sqlite_open($dbinfo['dbname'],0666,$errormessage);
      else
      $this->connection =
            sqlite_popen($dbinfo['dbname'],0666,$errormessage);
      if (!$this->connection)
      {
        throw new Exception($errormessage);
      }
    }
    else
    throw new Exception("You must supply database name for a
                                successful connection");
  }
  public function count()
  {
    $lastresult = $this->results[$this->lasthash];
    //print_r($this->results);
    $count = sqlite_num_rows($lastresult);
    if (!$count) $count = 0;
    return $count;
  }
  public function execute($sql)
  {
    $sql = $this->prepQuery($sql);
    $parts = split(" ",trim($sql));
    $type = strtolower($parts[0]);
    $hash = md5($sql);
    $this->lasthash = $hash;
    if ("select"==$type)
    {
```

```php
      if (isset($this->results[$hash]))
      {
        if (is_resource($this->results[$hash]))
        return $this->results[$hash];
      }
    }
    else if("update"==$type || "delete"==$type)
    {
      $this->results = array(); //clear the result cache
    }
    $this->results[$hash] = sqlite_query($sql,$this->connection);
  }
  private function prepQuery($sql)
  {
    return $sql;
  }
  public function escape($sql)
  {
    if (function_exists('sqlite_escape_string'))
    {
      return sqlite_escape_string($sql);
    }
    else
    {
      return addslashes($sql);
    }
  }
  public function affectedRows()
  {
    return sqlite_changes($this->connection);
  }
  public function insertId()
  {
    return @sqlite_last_insert_rowid($this->connection);
  }
  public function transBegin()
  {
    $this->execute('BEGIN TRANSACTION');
  }
  public function transCommit()
  {
    $this->execute('COMMIT');
  }
```

```php
  public function transRollback()
  {
    $this->execute('COMMIT');
  }
  public function getRow($fetchmode = FETCH_ASSOC)
  {
    $lastresult = $this->results[$this->lasthash];
    if (FETCH_ASSOC == $fetchmode)
    $row = sqlite_fetch_array($lastresult,SQLITE_ASSOC);
    elseif (FETCH_ROW == $fetchmode)
    $row = sqlite_fetch_array($lastresult, SQLITE_NUM);
    elseif (FETCH_OBJECT == $fetchmode)
    $row = sqlite_fetch_object($lastresult);
    else
    $row = sqlite_fetch_array($lastresult,SQLITE_BOTH);
    return $row;
  }
  public function getRowAt($offset=null,$fetchmode = FETCH_ASSOC)
  {
    $lastresult = $this->results[$this->lasthash];
    if (!empty($offset))
  {
      sqlite_seek($lastresult, $offset);
    }
    return $this->getRow($fetchmode);
  }
  public function rewind()
  {
    $lastresult = $this->results[$this->lasthash];
    sqlite_rewind($lastresult);
  }
  public function getRows($start, $count, $fetchmode = FETCH_ASSOC)
  {
    $lastresult = $this->results[$this->lasthash];
    sqlite_seek($lastresult, $start);
    $rows = array();
    for ($i=$start; $i<=($start+$count); $i++)
    {
      $rows[] = $this->getRow($fetchmode);
    }
    return $rows;
  }
}
?>
```

If you take a look at the code, you will find that we just implemented all the functions described in `abstractdbdriver` object in `abstractdbdriver.php`.

Here comes the driver file for MySQL, `core/main/dbdrivers/mysqldriver.php`:

```php
<?
class mysqldriver extends abstractdbdriver
{
  public function __construct($dbinfo)
  {
    if (!empty($dbinfo['dbname']))
    {
      if ($dbinfo['persistent'])
      $this->connection =
              mysql_pconnect($dbinfo['dbhost'],$dbinfo['dbuser'],
              $dbinfo['dbpwd']);
      else
      $this->connection =
              mysql_connect($dbinfo['dbhost'],$dbinfo['dbuser'],
              $dbinfo['dbpwd']);
      mysql_select_db($dbinfo['dbname'],$this->connection);
    }
    else
    throw new Exception("You must supply username, password,
            hostname and database name for connecting to mysql");
  }
  public function execute($sql)
  {
    $sql = $this->prepQuery($sql);
    $parts = split(" ",trim($sql));
    $type = strtolower($parts[0]);
    $hash = md5($sql);
    $this->lasthash = $hash;
    if ("select"==$type)
    {
      if (isset($this->results[$hash]))
      {
        if (is_resource($this->results[$hash]))
        return $this->results[$hash];
      }
    }
    else if("update"==$type || "delete"==$type)
    {
      $this->results = array(); //clear the result cache
```

```php
  }
  $this->results[$hash] = mysql_query($sql,$this->connection);
}
public function count()
{
  //print_r($this);
  $lastresult = $this->results[$this->lasthash];
  //print_r($this->results);
  $count = mysql_num_rows($lastresult);
  if (!$count) $count = 0;
  return $count;
}
private  function prepQuery($sql)
{
  // "DELETE FROM TABLE" returns 0 affected rows.
  // This hack modifies the query so that
  // it returns the number of affected rows
  if (preg_match('/^\s*DELETE\s+FROM\s+(\S+)\s*$/i', $sql))
  {
    $sql = preg_replace("/^\s*DELETE\s+FROM\s+(\S+)\s*$/",
                        "DELETE FROM \\1 WHERE 1=1", $sql);
  }
  return $sql;
}
public function escape($sql)
{
  if (function_exists('mysql_real_escape_string'))
  {
    return mysql_real_escape_string($sql, $this->conn_id);
  }
  elseif (function_exists('mysql_escape_string'))
  {
    return mysql_escape_string( $sql);
  }
  else
  {
    return addslashes($sql);
  }
}
public function affectedRows()
{
  return @mysql_affected_rows($this->connection);
}
```

```php
public function insertId()
{
  return @mysql_insert_id($this->connection);
}
public function transBegin()
{
  $this->execute('SET AUTOCOMMIT=0');
  $this->execute('START TRANSACTION'); // can also be BEGIN or
                                       // BEGIN WORK
  return TRUE;
}
public function transCommit()
{
  $this->execute('COMMIT');
  $this->execute('SET AUTOCOMMIT=1');
  return TRUE;
}
public function transRollback()
{
  $this->execute('ROLLBACK');
  $this->execute('SET AUTOCOMMIT=1');
  return TRUE;
}
public function getRow($fetchmode = FETCH_ASSOC)
{
  $lastresult = $this->results[$this->lasthash];
  if (FETCH_ASSOC == $fetchmode)
  $row = mysql_fetch_assoc($lastresult);
  elseif (FETCH_ROW == $fetchmode)
  $row = mysql_fetch_row($lastresult);
  elseif (FETCH_OBJECT == $fetchmode)
  $row = mysql_fetch_object($lastresult);
  else
  $row = mysql_fetch_array($lastresult,MYSQL_BOTH);
  return $row;
}
public function getRowAt($offset=null,$fetchmode = FETCH_ASSOC)
{
  $lastresult = $this->results[$this->lasthash];
  if (!empty($offset))
  {
    mysql_data_seek($lastresult, $offset);
  }
```

Chapter 9

```
    return $this->getRow($fetchmode);
  }
  public function rewind()
  {
    $lastresult = $this->results[$this->lasthash];
    mysql_data_seek($lastresult, 0);
  }
  public function getRows($start, $count, $fetchmode = FETCH_ASSOC)
  {
    $lastresult = $this->results[$this->lasthash];
    mysql_data_seek($lastresult, $start);
    $rows = array();
    for ($i=$start; $i<=($start+$count); $i++)
    {
      $rows[] = $this->getRow($fetchmode);
    }
    return $rows;
  }
  function __destruct(){
    foreach ($this->results as $result)
    {
      @mysql_free_result($result);
    }
  }
}
?>
```

And finally, here comes the PostgreSQL driver, core/main/dbdrivers/
postgresql.php:

```
<?
class pgsqldriver extends abstractdbdriver
{
  public function __construct($dbinfo)
  {
    if (!empty($dbinfo['dbname']))
    {
      if ($dbinfo['persistent'])
      $this->connection = pg_pconnect("host={$dbinfo['dbname']}
      port=5432 dbname={$dbinfo['dbname']} user={$dbinfo['$dbuser']}
      password={$dbinfo['dbpwd']}");
      else
      $this->connection = pg_connect("host={$dbinfo['dbname']}
      port=5432 dbname={$dbinfo['dbname']} user={$dbinfo['$dbuser']}
```

[237]

```
        password={$dbinfo['dbpwd']}");
    }
    else
    throw new Exception("You must supply username, password,
    hostname and database name for connecting to postgresql");
}
public function execute($sql)
{
    $sql = $this->prepQuery($sql);
    $parts = split(" ",trim($sql));
    $type = strtolower($parts[0]);
    $hash = md5($sql);
    $this->lasthash = $hash;
    if ("select"==$type)
    {
        if (isset($this->results[$hash]))
        {
            if (is_resource($this->results[$hash]))
            return $this->results[$hash];
        }
    }
    else if("update"==$type || "delete"==$type)
    {
        $this->results = array(); //clear the result cache
    }
    $this->results[$hash] = pg_query($this->connection,$sql);
}
public function count()
{
    //print_r($this);
    $lastresult = $this->results[$this->lasthash];
    //print_r($this->results);
    $count = pg_num_rows($lastresult);
    if (!$count) $count = 0;
    return $count;
}
private function prepQuery($sql)
{
    // "DELETE FROM TABLE" returns 0 affected rows this hack modifies
    // the query so that it returns the number of affected rows
    if (preg_match('/^\s*DELETE\s+FROM\s+(\S+)\s*$/i', $sql))
    {
        $sql = preg_replace("/^\s*DELETE\s+FROM\s+(\S+)\s*$/",
```

```
                         "DELETE FROM \\1 WHERE 1=1", $sql);
    }
    return $sql;
  }
  public function escape($sql)
  {
    if (function_exists('pg_escape_string'))
    {
      return pg_escape_string( $sql);
    }
    else
    {
      return addslashes($sql);
    }
  }
  public function affectedRows()
  {
    return @pg_affected_rows($this->connection);
  }
  public function insertId($table=null, $column=null)
  {
    $_temp = $this->lasthash;
    $lastresult = $this->results[$this->lasthash];
    $this->execute("SELECT version() AS ver");
    $row = $this->getRow();
    $v = $row['server'];
    $table = func_num_args() > 0 ? func_get_arg(0) : null;
    $column = func_num_args() > 1 ? func_get_arg(1) : null;
    if ($table == null && $v >= '8.1')
    {
      $sql='SELECT LASTVAL() as ins_id';
    }
    elseif ($table != null && $column != null && $v >= '8.0')
    {
      $sql = sprintf("SELECT pg_get_serial_sequence('%s','%s') as
                                        seq", $table, $column);
      $this->execte($sql);
      $row = $this->getRow();
      $sql = sprintf("SELECT CURRVAL('%s') as ins_id", $row['seq']);
    }
    elseif ($table != null)
    {
      // seq_name passed in table parameter
```

```
      $sql = sprintf("SELECT CURRVAL('%s') as ins_id", $table);
    }
    else
    {
      return pg_last_oid($lastresult);
    }
    $this->execute($sql);
    $row = $this->getRow();
    $this->lasthash = $_temp;
    return $row['ins_id'];
  }
  public function transBegin()
  {
    return @pg_exec($this->connection, "BEGIN");
    return TRUE;
  }
  public function transCommit()
  {
    return @pg_exec($this->connection, "COMMIT");
    return TRUE;
  }
  public function transRollback()
  {
    return @pg_exec($this->connection, "ROLLBACK");
    return TRUE;
  }
  public function getRow($fetchmode = FETCH_ASSOC)
  {
    $lastresult = $this->results[$this->lasthash];
    if (FETCH_ASSOC == $fetchmode)
    $row = pg_fetch_assoc($lastresult);
    elseif (FETCH_ROW == $fetchmode)
    $row = pg_fetch_row($lastresult);
    elseif (FETCH_OBJECT == $fetchmode)
    $row = pg_fetch_object($lastresult);
    else
    $row = pg_fetch_array($lastresult,PGSQL_BOTH);
    return $row;
  }
  public function getRowAt($offset=null,$fetchmode = FETCH_ASSOC)
  {
    $lastresult = $this->results[$this->lasthash];
    if (!empty($offset))
```

```
    {
        pg_result_seek($lastresult, $offset);
    }
    return $this->getRow($fetchmode);
  }
  public function rewind()
  {
    $lastresult = $this->results[$this->lasthash];
    pg_result_seek($lastresult, 0);
  }
  public function getRows($start, $count, $fetchmode = FETCH_ASSOC)
  {
    $lastresult = $this->results[$this->lasthash];
    $rows = array();
    for ($i=$start; $i<=($start+$count); $i++)
    {
        $rows[] = $this->getRowAt($i,$fetchmode);
    }
    return $rows;
  }
  function __destruct(){
    foreach ($this->results as $result)
    {
        @pg_free_result($result);
    }
  }
 }
}
?>
```

Now our framework is done. In the coming sections, we will see how to build applications over this framework.

Building Applications over our Framework

Now is the colourful moment. So far, we have done so many things to ease developing applications over our framework. So now in this section we will develop a basic blog application and discuss how to take advantage of our framework.

For those unfamiliar with Blogs, they are simply web-based publishing systems, where people are allowed to write anything and publish it. In this application we will allow users to write articles, display them, and also allow users to publish comments.

Let's create a MySQL database named `packtblog` with three tables; `Users`, `Posts`, and `Comments`. Here is the database schema:

```
Table: Posts
+---------+--------------+------+-----+---------+----------------+
| Field   | Type         | Null | Key | Default | Extra          |
+---------+--------------+------+-----+---------+----------------+
| id      | int(11)      | NO   | PRI | NULL    | auto_increment |
| title   | varchar(250) | YES  |     | NULL    |                |
| content | text         | YES  |     | NULL    |                |
| user_id | int(11)      | YES  |     | NULL    |                |
| date    | int(11)      | YES  |     | NULL    |                |
+---------+--------------+------+-----+---------+----------------+

Table: Comments
+---------+--------------+------+-----+---------+----------------+
| Field   | Type         | Null | Key | Default | Extra          |
+---------+--------------+------+-----+---------+----------------+
| id      | int(11)      | NO   | PRI | NULL    | auto_increment |
| post_id | int(11)      | YES  |     | NULL    |                |
| content | text         | YES  |     | NULL    |                |
| date    | int(11)      | YES  |     | NULL    |                |
| author  | varchar(250) | YES  |     | NULL    |                |
+---------+--------------+------+-----+---------+----------------+

Table: Users
+----------+--------------+------+-----+---------+----------------+
| Field    | Type         | Null | Key | Default | Extra          |
+----------+--------------+------+-----+---------+----------------+
| id       | int(11)      | NO   | PRI | NULL    | auto_increment |
| name     | varchar(100) | YES  |     | NULL    |                |
| fullname | varchar(250) | YES  |     | NULL    |                |
| email    | varchar(250) | YES  |     | NULL    |                |
| password | varchar(32)  | YES  |     | NULL    |                |
+----------+--------------+------+-----+---------+----------------+
```

Authentication Controller

Let's design our main controller with users who, will be able to register, or log into, their system. The code in the `app/controllers/auth.php` file is as follows:

```
<?
session_start();
class auth extends controller
```

```
{
  public $use_layout = false;
  function base()
  {
  }
  public function login()
  {
    //$this->redirect("auth");
    $this->view->set("message","");
    if(!empty($_SESSION['userid']))
    {
      $this->redirect("blog","display");
    }
    else if (!empty($_POST))
    {
      $user = $this->model->user;
      $userdata = $user->find(array("name"=>$user->name,
                       "password"=>md5($user->password)));
      if (!$userdata)
      {
        //not found
        $this->view->set("message","Wrong username and password");
      }
      else
      {
        $_SESSION['userid']=$userdata['id'];
        $this->redirect("blog","display");
      }
    }
  }
  public function register()
  {
    if(!empty($_POST)){
      $user = $this->model->user;
      if (!$user->find(array("name"=>$user->name))){
        $user->password = md5($user->password);
        $user->insert();
      }
    }
  }
}
?>
```

Here are the views for authentication controller:

app/views/auth/base.php

```
<h1>
   Please <a href='<?=$base_url?>/auth/login'>login</a> or
          <a href='<?=$base_url?>/auth/register'>register</a>
</h1>
```

This will display the following screen:

Please login or register

app/views/auth/login.php

```
<h1>Please login</h1>
<font color="red"><?=$message;?></font><br/>
<form method="POST">
   Username:<br/>
   <input type="text" name="name"/><br/>
   Password: <br/>
   <input type="password" name="password" /><br/>
   <input type="submit" name="Submit" value="Login" />
</form>
```

This will display the following screen:

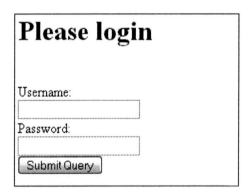

app/views/auth/register.php

```
<h1>Please register your account</h1><br/>
<form method="POST">
   Your username: <br/>
   <input type="text" name="name" /><br/>
   Password: <br/>
   <input type="password" name="password" /><br/>
```

```
  Fullname: <br/>
  <input type="text" name="fullname" /><br/>
  Email: <br/>
  <input type="text" name="email" /><br/>
  <input type="submit"  name="submit" value="Register"/>
</form>
```

This will display the following screen:

Now comes the controller which will handle the blog operations

The code in the app/controllers/blog.php is as follows:

```
<?
session_start();
class blog extends controller
{
  public function display()
  {
    $user = $_SESSION['userid'];
    $posts = $this->model->post->find(array("user_id"=>$user),10);
    if(!$posts)
    {
      $this->redirect("blog","write");
    }
    else
    {
      foreach ($posts as &$post)
      {
        $post['comments']=$this->model->comment->find
                          (array("post_id"=>$post['id']));
      }
      $this->view->set("posts",$posts);
```

```php
      }
    }
    public function post()
    {
      $postid= $this->params['0'];
      if (count($_POST)>1)
      {
        $comment = $this->model->comment;
        $comment->date = time();
        $comment->post_id = $postid;
        $comment->insert();
      }
      $post = $this->model->post->find(array("id"=>$postid));
      if (!empty($postid))
      {
        $post[0]['comments'] = $this->model->comment->find
                              (array("post_id"=>$postid),100);
      }
      $this->view->set("message","");
      $this->view->set("post",$post[0]);
      //die($postid);

    }
    public function write()
    {
      $this->view->set("color","green");
      if (!empty($_POST))
      {
        $post = $this->model->post;
        $post->user_id=$_SESSION['userid'];
        $post->date = time();
        $post->insert();
        $this->view->set("color","green");
        $this->view->set("message","Successfully saved
                                        your blog post");
      }
    }
  }
?>
```

And here are the views of our blog controller:

app/views/blog/display.php

```php
<?
foreach ($posts as $post)
{
  echo "<div id='post{$post['id']}' >";
  echo "<b><a href='{$base_url}/blog/post/{$post['id']}'>
                        {$post['title']}</a></b><br/>";
  echo "<p>".nl2br($post['content'])."</p>";
  echo "Number of comments: ".(count($post['comments']));
  echo "</div>";
}
?>
```

app/views/blog/post.php

```php
<?
  echo "<div id='post{$post['id']}' >";
  echo "<b><a href='{$base_url}/blog/post/{$post['id']}'>
                        {$post['title']}</a></b><br/>";
  echo "<p>".nl2br($post['content'])."</p>";
  echo "Number of comments: ".(count($post['comments']));
  echo "</div>";
  foreach ($post['comments'] as $comment)
  {
    echo "<div style='padding:10px;margin-top:10px;
    border:1px solid #cfcfcf;'>";
    $time = date("Y-m-d",$comment['date']);
    echo "Posted by {$comment['author']} at {$time}:<br/>";
    echo "{$comment['content']}";
    echo "</div>";
  }
?>
<h2>Post a new comment</h2>
<font color="red"><?=$message;?></font><br/>
<form method="POST">
  Name:<br/>
  <input type="text" name="author"/><br/>
  Comment: <br/>
  <textarea rows="5" cols="60" name="content" ></textarea><br/>
  <input type="submit" />
</form>
```

```
app/views/blog/write.php
<h1>Write a new blog post</h1>
<font color="<?=$color;?>"><?=$message;?></font><br/>
<form method="POST">
  Title:<br/>
  <input type="text" name="title"/><br/>
  Content: <br/>
  <textarea rows="5" cols="60" name="content" ></textarea><br/>
  <input type="submit" value="save"  />
</form>
```

This will display the following form:

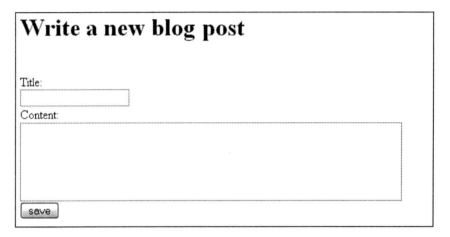

And last but not the least here comes the config file. Place it in
app/config/configs.php or core/config/configs.php:

```
<?
$configs['use_layout']=false;
$configs['unit_test_enabled']=true;
$configs['default_controller']="welcome";
$configs['global_profile']=true;
/* DB */
$configs['db']['usedb']="mysql";
$configs['db']['development']['dbname']="packtblog";
$configs['db']['development']['dbhost']="localhost";
$configs['db']['development']['dbuser']="root";
$configs['db']['development']['dbpwd']="root1234";
$configs['db']['development']['persistent']=true;
$configs['db']['development']['dbtype']="mysql";
?>
```

Summary

In the rapid development of PHP applications, frameworks play a very important role. That is why today there are so many enterprise-level frameworks in the market and you have so many choices. We have learnt how to build a framework in this chapter which will also help to understand object loading, data abstraction layers, and the importance of separation. Finally, we took a closer look at how applications are done.

Index

Packt Open Source Project Royalties

When we sell a book written on an Open Source project, we pay a royalty directly to that project. Therefore by purchasing Object-Oriented Programming with PHP5, Packt will have given some of the money received to the PHP project.

In the long term, we see ourselves and you — customers and readers of our books — as part of the Open Source ecosystem, providing sustainable revenue for the projects we publish on. Our aim at Packt is to establish publishing royalties as an essential part of the service and support a business model that sustains Open Source.

If you're working with an Open Source project that you would like us to publish on, and subsequently pay royalties to, please get in touch with us.

Writing for Packt

We welcome all inquiries from people who are interested in authoring. Book proposals should be sent to authors@packtpub.com. If your book idea is still at an early stage and you would like to discuss it first before writing a formal book proposal, contact us; one of our commissioning editors will get in touch with you.

We're not just looking for published authors; if you have strong technical skills but no writing experience, our experienced editors can help you develop a writing career, or simply get some additional reward for your expertise.

About Packt Publishing

Packt, pronounced 'packed', published its first book "Mastering phpMyAdmin for Effective MySQL Management" in April 2004 and subsequently continued to specialize in publishing highly focused books on specific technologies and solutions.

Our books and publications share the experiences of your fellow IT professionals in adapting and customizing today's systems, applications, and frameworks. Our solution-based books give you the knowledge and power to customize the software and technologies you're using to get the job done. Packt books are more specific and less general than the IT books you have seen in the past. Our unique business model allows us to bring you more focused information, giving you more of what you need to know, and less of what you don't.

Packt is a modern, yet unique publishing company, which focuses on producing quality, cutting-edge books for communities of developers, administrators, and newbies alike. For more information, please visit our website: www.PacktPub.com.

Learning PHP Data Objects

ISBN: 978-1-847192-66-0   Paperback: 200 pages

A Beginner's Guide to PHP Data Objects, Database Connection Abstraction Library for PHP 5

1. An overview of PDO

2. Creating a database and connecting to it

3. Error Handling

4. Advanced features

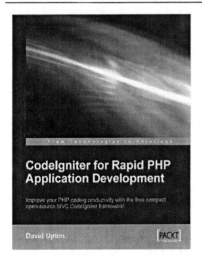

CodeIgniter for Rapid PHP Application Development

ISBN: 978-1-847191-74-8   Paperback: 220 pages

Improve your PHP coding productivity with the free compact open-source MVC CodeIgniter framework!

1. Clear, structured tutorial on working with CodeIgniter

2. Careful explanation of the basic concepts of CodeIgniter and its MVC architecture

3. Using CodeIgniter with databases, HTML forms, files, images, sessions, and email

4. Building a dynamic website quickly and easily using CodeIgniter's prepared code

Please check **www.PacktPub.com** for information on our titles

PHP Oracle Web Development

ISBN: 978-1-847193-63-6   Paperback: 350 pages

A practical guide to combining the power, performance, scalability, and reliability of the Oracle Database with the ease of use, short development time, and high performance of PHP

1. Program your own PHP/Oracle application

2. Move data processing inside the database

3. Distribute data processing between the web/PHP and Oracle database servers

4. Create reusable building blocks for PHP/Oracle solutions

5. Use up-to-date technologies, such as Ajax and web services, in PHP Oracle development

Smarty PHP Template Programming and Applications

ISBN: 1-904811-40-X   Paperback: 250 pages

A step-by-step guide to building PHP web sites and applications using the Smarty templating engine

1. Bring the benefits of Smarty to your PHP programming

2. Give your designers the power to modify content and layout without PHP programming

3. Produce code that is easier to debug, maintain, and modify

4. Useful for both Smarty developers and users

Please check **www.PacktPub.com** for information on our titles

Printed in the United Kingdom
by Lightning Source UK Ltd.
125973UK00001B/95/A